Upscaling Earth

Anna Heringer
Lindsay Blair Howe
Martin Rauch

UPSCALING EARTH

MATERIAL
PROCESS
CATALYST

Second edition

gta Verlag

Foreword 6
Annette Spiro

The Case for Earth 16
Reframing Sustainable Building 28
Material 43
Process 60
Catalyst 111
A Roadmap for Upscaling 126

Author Biographies 156
Illustration Credits 158

Foreword

Annette Spiro

Swiss travel writer René Gardi's book *Indigenous African Architecture*[1] was originally published in Bern in 1973. I was immediately fascinated by his images of the artful earthen dwellings in West Africa long before I developed an interest in architecture. Later, once I began studying the subject, earth was not a part of our curriculum—nor did this book from my youth conform to the clear lines of modernism we were taught. Architects who practiced earth building were treated with skepticism. Today, the opposite is true. When the authors of this book began teaching at the ETH Zurich in 2014, their studio design course on earthen architecture was full immediately. What lies behind this shift and what captured the imagination of these aspiring architects? Was it the allure of this archaic material? Or was it the prospect of a future shaped by resource scarcity, in which the building materials we take for granted are no longer widely available? In the meantime, students in Europe—and around the world—have begun staging protests and demanding decisive action to protect the climate. Is it not tempting to presume these things are connected? Or, after decades of hearing that "anything goes" in architecture, do students perhaps yearn for an architecture related to its construction, inherently grounded in its materials?

When Anna Heringer and Martin Rauch were appointed to the ETH Zurich, their projects had long served to refute this aforementioned skepticism about earthen architecture. Buildings such as Haus Rauch, the Ricola Kräuterzentrum, or the Modern Education and Training Institute (METI) School in Bangladesh silenced earth's critics and proved how much architectonic and structural potential the world's oldest building material possesses. These projects rely on the fundamentals of earth building that have existed for centuries. Craftsmen and builders all over the world developed their own unique culture of earth building, mastered and perfected over countless generations. This resulted in the kind of knowledge that exists in the minds and hands of craftsmen, and in buildings themselves, rather than in books. Until recently, earthen architecture was not part of the architectural curriculum. The authors of this book obtained their knowledge on their own—analyzing ancient building tools, gaining experience on building sites, working with craftsmen in Europe, Africa, and Asia—conducting empirical as well as scientific experiments with the material itself. As such, it is even more important and valuable that this knowledge has been made available to all of us in *Upscaling Earth*. Anna Heringer, Lindsay Blair Howe, and Martin Rauch show that looking back to this age-old tradition is also looking toward the future.

Earth building is not a rapid construction method—it takes time. However, the material can be found almost anywhere and extracted for very little cost. Soon, material, not time, will be our most precious commodity. This is my hope, and it would greatly benefit architecture. Architecture has always maximized whatever time is available. But who knows if time may not soon be in abundant rather than in short supply? Could the supposed drawbacks of a slower building process even become a significant asset? Fortunately, our authors have not simply waited for these things to unfold, but are developing groundbreaking, rational techniques for earth building. Prefabricated elements of rammed earth, as for example implemented in a cupola for the ETH Zurich or the Ricola Kräuterzentrum in Basel, are new both in their form and scale.

The impact of this approach on architectural form and expression is not yet clear. New building techniques have not always automatically led to new kinds of built forms. The vaults of Gothic cathedrals did not achieve such great heights because their stonemasons were highly skilled, but because they conceptualized space anew. Their relentless determination to execute their vision allowed the builders and masons to create these dizzying structural masterpieces. The opposite is true of concrete. The first reinforced concrete buildings resembled masonry, and the full architectonic and spatial potentials of this new technology—casting the concrete—developed gradually. Even earthen architecture does not always reveal its process. In contrast to traditional earth building in Africa or the Middle East, the structures of rainy Northern and Central Europe were often masked by layers of plastering; their form did not indicate their method of construction. Nevertheless, earth building is strongly characterized by its structural principles. The limits imposed by the material are even more true for rammed earth than for more "flexible" earthen techniques, such as adobe bricks. Since non-reinforced rammed earth only functions in compression, elements such as roofing or filigree construction details were inconceivable until very recently. Modular systems have now unlocked previously unimaginable possibilities. In the future, rammed earth components could even be capable of spanning large spaces. And then there are digital tools. They are rendering standardization in prefabricated parts obsolete, and they allow the creation of customized elements. Between industrial manufacturing and craftsmanship may even lie a third option, in which handmade and digital tools interact. Or, as with the Gothic churches, the building site could once again become the locus of production.

Whoever thinks that earth building is slow to progress—like evolution—is missing the point. Behind the advances in earthen architecture, and behind its most celebrated masterpieces, is not just a centuries-old tradition. Pioneers and ambitious inventors dared to test something new. That includes the authors of this book! Designing and building with earth requires ingenuity, a passion for experimentation, and this is why it should be a part of our education. It is a fascinating subject for future architects— for it is they who must solve problems unforeseen. They are still open-minded, and approach this ancient material with the same curiosity and adventuresome spirit with which they welcome the newest technologies.

1   René Gardi, *Indigenous African Architecture*, trans. from German by Sigrid MacRae (London: Van Nostrand Reinhold, 1975). Interestingly, the original German title was much more complex: *Auch im Lehmhaus lässt sich's leben: Über traditionelles Bauen und Wohnen in Westafrika* (Life in a Mud House Is Also Possible: On Traditional Building and Living in West Africa).

This book is a collective work by the three authors, highlighting both shared experiences and individual stories about designing and building with earth. Personal narratives by an individual author are graphically indented and designated with their initials: A.H. for Anna Heringer, L.B.H. for Lindsay Blair Howe, and M.R. for Martin Rauch.

Opposite pages:

10 Earthen city of Shibam in Yemen.
11 Haus Rauch in Schlins, Austria.

12 Staircase at Haus Rauch.
13 Plazza Pintgia Stable in Almens, Switzerland.

14 OMICRON monolith in Klaus, Austria.
15 Exhibition at Haus der Architektur in Graz, Austria.

The Case for Earth

We, the authors of this book, are trained in the arts of building and educating. The acute challenges facing our planet have forced us to fundamentally question our building cultures, both locally and globally, as we contend with the privileges and paradigms of creating architecture. How can we, and our future generations, sustain the planet while building for an ever-growing population? Are we going to be a part of the problem or a part of the solution?

According to recent reports by the WWF[1] and Global Footprint Network,[2] if everyone on earth continued to live as we do today, we would require between one and six whole worlds in order to sustain the needs of the current global population, including the provision of resources as well as the removal of waste. Analysis of these reports by *Die Welt* newspaper even predicted that three worlds would already be required to meet the needs of the projected population as early as 2050.[3] Fortunately, however, a sense of "ecologization" has begun to permeate the Anthropocene, from the sharing economy to social media activism and consumer responsibility. As architects and developers, economists and sociologists, international organizations and local communities—whichever labels we apply to ourselves—we have all become increasingly aware of the significant impact we have on the environment and are seeking more ecological approaches to design and construction.

One of the most prescient solutions for more sustainable building is to use natural, untreated earth from the ground. Earth is one of the most widely available and venerated materials in human history. But it is not just a building material; it is a process, and a catalyst. Earth is a *Weltanschauung*. Supremely local and sustainable, there is no other material which can be recycled time and time again without a loss in quality; which does not release any carbon dioxide in its production; which maintains the perfect indoor humid-

An ecological approach to building is supported by sustainable materials such as earth, used in the Mezzana Agricultural School (2010–2012) in Switzerland. Concept by Conte Pianetti Zanetta Architetti and Lehm Ton Erde GmbH.

House in Flims, Switzerland (2011). Architecture by FeBruAr and earth building executed by Lehm Ton Erde Baukunst GmbH.

ity and absorbs smells; which creates pleasant acoustics; which can bear structural loads and act as a thermal mass; which has a plethora of aesthetic design possibilities; and which has no negative externalities for humankind in its production process, its implementation, and its maintenance. However, in order for earth to fulfill its potential, it has to be *upscaled*: it must meet the contemporary demands of sustainable architectural design, and it must be possible to implement across a variety of social, economic, and environmental conditions. This book outlines the path we ourselves—as three practitioners of design education and proponents of earth as a material, a process, and a catalyst—envision for this *upscaling*.

Appropriate Building

Building is intimately connected to our planet and its inhabitants. Even in its most simplistic, archaic forms, the act of building requires both human labor as well as the substances of the earth. The tools and methods of construction began to evolve as soon as human beings first made shelter to protect themselves from the elements: simple structures, handcrafted solutions with the materials available from the surrounding environment. In the meantime, the manifold approaches to building possible today, when urbanization has reached a planetary scale, have become increasingly complex, ranging from highly sustainable projects to those which inflict significant negative externalities on the environment, the economy, and society. Even a simple project can actively impede sustainable development, for example by utilizing imported and environmentally harmful materials. A complex project, on the other hand, can equally promote multiple forms of sustainability, for example by incorporating local materials and employing local populations in the design process. In the face of climate change, resource scarcity, and shifting populations, how can we define sustainability? And how ought our practices and methods contribute to a more sustainable future?

Consider the process of creating the fifteenth-century Inca citadel of Machu Picchu in Peru—a fascinating example of architectural design and sustainable planning. The most common way to approach the site today is departing the city of Cuzco by train, snaking through an ancient agricultural landscape. The vast majority of homes along this path from the city into the Andes are constructed with earth: adobe walls laid on fieldstone foundations, executed as they have been for centuries. Simple yet robust dwellings, they were not intended to be permanent and could be simply folded back into the ground when no longer required. However, in their holiest of places at Machu Picchu, the Incas constructed dry masonry walls of unparalleled proportions. The buildings themselves varied in the effort and skill required, from aligning uncut stones to multiple forms of polygonal and coursed

The Temple of the Sun illustrates the manifold possibilities of working with a single building material, upscaling stone for the holy structure of Machu Picchu in Peru.

masonry, culminating in the intricate carvings of the Temple of the Sun, where natural rock is supplemented with meticulously cut stones. The entire site was holistically designed according to rainfall and runoff, to the extent that it was largely self-sustaining. There is a twofold lesson embedded in the Inca practices of settlement creation: fully exploiting material properties and building appropriately.

For contemporary practices in the built environment, this means that we should upscale our materials and techniques to appropriately match the social, economic, and environmental contexts of our building task. Precisely because earth, too, can be elevated as a material and edified as a process to many degrees, it represents one of the most transcendent solutions for sustainable design today. Every project presents a challenge in regard to the balance between human labor and technology, and the use of earth can be adjusted to meet the needs of the program and match the materials available. As such, it is possible for earth to function as a viable building material across the spectrum of design, from the simple or ephemeral to the complex and permanent.

The Potential of Earth

Earth can serve as the basis for infinite conceptualizations and take on many colors and forms. From a historical perspective, earth is our oldest and single most important building material; it encapsulates qualities that anchor architecture in its very roots. As Kjetil Trædal Thorsen, founder of the Snøhetta design practice, has noted:

> The essence of creation is captured in one material as old as the world itself and brand new as fast as it dries. It is as warm as the color tones of the ground it comes from, as hard as rock to equally withstand the forces that made it, controlling humidity, temperature. Show me one other material that can do the same.[4]

Earth can be found almost anywhere in the world and translated into a contextually unique structure. Whether in the desert climates of North Africa, the tropical monsoon regions of Asia, or the frost-laden contexts of Central Europe; whether a peripheral single-family residence or highly urban, multistory building: earth is both a viable and palpably sustainable material with which to design our world.

Archeological excavations have revealed that earth has consistently been one of the most widely used building materials, traversing climates and continents, and that the building culture of earth has existed for more than nine thousand years.[5] Its typologies include not just residential structures but the religious buildings, statues, and monuments, the ziggurats and fortifications that remain a part of the urbanized world today. The cities of Jericho, Chan-Chan in Peru, or Babylon in Iraq, the Alhambra in Spain, and even the original parts of the Great Wall of China were all constructed using various earth building techniques, from adobe brickmaking to ramming.[6] Three thousand two hundred years ago, parts of the temple complex of Ramses II were constructed with earth bricks in Gourna, Egypt; the core of the sun pyramid in Teotihuacán, Mexico, was primarily constructed with rammed earth between the years 300 and 900 CE.[7] Moreover, the earthen elements of these edifices did not contain any form of further structural reinforcement

The Case for Earth

City of Shibam in Yemen, built in earth in the sixteenth century.

or stabilization beyond wooden ring beams or lintels of stone. These works demonstrate the ability of earth to withstand the tests of time and—particularly when well maintained—to survive weather events and even natural disasters such as earthquakes.

Currently, earth is the only material that completely aligns with fully sustainable building principles, such as the cradle-to-cradle concept.[8] Like no other building material, earth is not only suited to its local climate but also has the capacity to generate an equally localized building culture, one in which investments in construction are grounded in social capital. It is this key aspect that gives earthen architecture the potential to break the cycles of financialization that extract profits from localities to enrich global conglomerates and corporations, and that so often dictate the course of development around the globe. Instead, the ever-varying characteristics of earth promote a broad range of socially sustainable and economically viable solutions.

More than this, earth also provides a rich aesthetic palette that mirrors and expresses cultural diversity. Anyone who has stood inside a house made of earth is familiar with the strong sense of place the material generates. Earth is healthy, not just in regard to sustainable construction, but also in the sense of physical and psychological well-being. It creates an emotional, familiar atmosphere and an unparalleled interior climate. While earth itself is not technologically advanced, it is capable of highly technical feats; for example, its ability to absorb water vapor like no other human-made material. Elevated and edified or not, earth contains great potential to meet contemporary needs. As described by Iranian-American architect Mohsen Mostafavi: "The limitations of a material's use, or mis-use, depend solely on our capacity to imagine alternative and unexpected means of incorporating it into the design process."[9]

Architecture, as a design practice, began to eschew building with earth hundreds of years ago. The evolving specialization of the design world and fascination with more technologically advanced methods has relegated earth to a primitive, basic material. Only recently has this perception begun to change, and the potentials of one of our most ancient building materials explored anew. The challenge, therefore, as formulated by Mostafavi, is: "How can we use dirt from the surface of the earth to make an alternative architecture that is both technically and aesthetically responsive to the conditions of our times?"[10]

Who Profits?

At the crux of the argument for using natural materials like earth lies the question of who profits. There are both environmental and societal consequences for the overuse of fossil-fuel-based substances like cement, and the use of earth can act to discourage their deployment. Potentially in combination with other materials such as timber, concrete, or steel, earth can form a hybrid structural system that results in an environmentally, economically, and culturally appropriate architectonic solution for any given context.

Our current resources must suffice for more than seven and a half billion people to date. Concrete and steel alone cannot house continuing population growth. Beyond the scarcity of resources that we face in the future, it is also predicted that mass labor employment will decline, particularly in the building and manufacturing sectors as they are currently structured. The American economist Jeremy Rifkin, for instance, anticipates an end of wage labor in industrial production: "The new high-tech revolutions of the 21st century end mass wage labor—meaning the cheapest worker in the world is more expensive than the intelligent technology coming online to replace them." He concludes: "We have to explore bold new approaches to addressing the problems created by the phenomenon of the disappearance of mass labor."[11]

In contrast, by shifting priorities, the building sector could instead contribute significantly to the future demands for work and wage labor. Therefore, the most significant benefit in upscaling earth is its potential to meet these needs, in any given situation, and its theoretical ability to balance the factors of labor, production costs, gray energy, water use, and the transportation of resources to create fair opportunities. So why is it not more commonly implemented?

First and foremost, there is no lobby for earth—primarily because it can be financialized at a significantly lower level than materials that have to be imported and are purportedly longer lasting. Imagery in the modern age is compelling and is transmitted globally by powerful entities. Concrete, for example, is still all too often portrayed as the material of progress—a panacea for under-resourced and underprivileged areas.

Furthermore, for instance among agricultural populations of Bangladesh or Peru, this inferior status is because vernacular earthen structures are associated with poverty, whereas industrialized materials like concrete, steel, and glass represent modernity, progress, and opportunity. Concrete-block, single-family homes have been the dream and the benchmark of advancement for generations, driven in turn by international development projects sponsored and financed by powerful corporate interests. Earth, in contrast, is perceived as fragile, ephemeral, and sometimes even as dangerous. This conception of earth as a material for low-income construction, as an unglamorous and even backward way of living, also continues to preclude its wider use. It undercuts the potentially much more beneficial efforts and ad-

Pretoria Portland Cement (PPC) is one of the largest producers of cement and aggregates in Southern Africa, where their iconic elephant logo is practically synonymous with development work.

vances that could be made with traditional materials or building practices, particularly in under-resourced contexts, to retain profits within local cycles of production. The necessity of sustaining the planet for both current and future generations urgently requires alternative, locally based, and low-carbon solutions for the building industry.

Upscaling Earth

Upscaling can be defined as improving the quality or value of a substance or, alternatively, an increase in its scale. In this book, we employ both senses of the term, and they are interlinked: in order to increase the scale of using earth as a progressive, forward-thinking building material, both the material itself as well as how it is implemented must continue to be improved.

A new wave of innovation is framing earth as a potential solution to the urgent problem of sustainable building, precisely because of its capacity to oscillate between industrialized production and human-powered construction, suiting a wide range of climates and cultures. The work of the Pritzker Prize-winning architect Wang Shu, the Ricola Kräuterzentrum designed by architects Herzog & de Meuron, the 2016 Venice Biennale curated by Alejandro Aravena, and the numerous recent publications on the use of rammed earth are all testimonies to the growing profile of earth. However, this recognition raises the question as to how a material that has traditionally relied so heavily on local substance and personal experience can be appropriately upscaled.

As a material, earth can be elevated to align with the entire spectrum of sustainable construction, from low-tech to high-tech, and as a process it can edify local practices and engender social development. Yet earth is more than this—it embodies a fundamentally different attitude toward design and building. It is an emancipatory endeavor and, ideally, a catalyst for a more sustainable world. We ourselves do not just want to promote earth as a building material; rather, we are involved in encouraging a dissemination of knowledge about the processes behind turning earth into a building material suited to local resources and requirements.

How do we want to live? What are our dreams for how we shape the world around us? Where do these impressions come from, and how can we move from our current realities toward these visions? This book is dedicated to exploring these questions in terms of building with earth. Through discussion of the fundamental principles behind earth as a material, a process, and a catalyst, we attempt to delineate what is necessary in order for upscaling to occur. The book first probes the appropriateness of earth, including the stigmas and challenges attached to it. It then delves deeper into the topic of technological innovation, primarily in regard to prefabrication. Using a spectrum of built and unbuilt works, from the remote villages of Africa to the metropolises of Europe, it illustrates how upscaling has been incrementally evolving. A particular focus is placed on rammed earth, assessing its potentials and risks. Finally, it outlines economic and social factors that could precipitate this transition. It concludes with a roadmap of what is necessary to conduct mass upscaling, including normative, institutional, and design-based perspectives.

We are not attempting to create a compendium about how to build with earth, nor to compile a history of earthen architecture. In an age of instant communication spanning a completely urbanized planet, a part of each and every one of us longs for a connection to our environment, to the archaic image of building—to the earth. It is through this image and through our experiences as practitioners and educators that we set out to envision the future of sustainable building and earthen architecture.

1   World Wildlife Fund (WWF), *Living Planet Report 2012: Biodiversity, Biocapacity* (Gland: WWF International, 2012), pp. 9–12. The more recent 2018 *Living Planet Report* confirms these findings, emphasizing that nature is the basis for human flourishing and economic activity, and highlighting the urgency of addressing chains of production and consumption. See World Wildlife Fund (WWF), *Living Planet Report 2018: Aiming Higher* (Gland: WWF International, 2018), p. 5.
2   Global Footprint Network (GFN), "Ecological Footprint," http://www.footprintnetwork.org/en/index.php/GFN/page/world_footprint/ (accessed September 8, 2018).
3   Alexandra Stahl, "Weltbevölkerung braucht Ressourcen von drei Erden," *Die Welt Online*, January 11, 2012, https://www.welt.de/wissenschaft/article13809375/Welt-bevoelkerung-braucht-Ressourcen-von-drei-Erden.html (accessed September 8, 2018).
4   Kjetil Trædal Thorsen, as location in Venice in "Mud WORKS!" poster for the 15th International Architecture Exhibition, *Biennale architettura 2016: Reporting from the Front*, May 28 to November 27, 2016.
5   See Gernot Minke, *Building with Earth: Design and Technology of a Sustainable Architecture* (Basel: Birkhäuser, 2012, 3rd ed.), p. 11.
6   See David Easton, *The Rammed Earth House* (White River Junction: Chelsea Green Publishing, 2007), p. 4.
7   Ibid. pp. 3–9.
8   See William McDonough and Michael Braungart, *Cradle to Cradle: Remaking the Way We Make Things* (New York: North Point Press, 2002).
9   Mohsen Mostafavi, as cited in "Mud WORKS!" (see note 4).
10 Ibid.
11 Jeremy Rifkin, "The End of Work," *Spiegel Online,* August 3, 2005, https://www.spiegel.de/international/jeremy-rifkin-on-europe-s-uncertain-future-the-end-of-work-a-368155.html (accessed December 22, 2018). See also Jeremy Rifkin, *The End of Work: The Decline of the Global Labor Force and the Dawn of the Post-market Era* (New York: Putnam Publishing Group, 1995).

Reframing Sustainable Building

Northern Bangladesh, from above, resembles a woven green-and-brown tapestry: the rhythmic green of rice paddies dotted with ponds and mounds of earth—the primary source of local building material. While in its urban centralities Bangladesh is the most densely populated nation on the planet, these outlying areas remain comparatively frozen in time. Few opportunities beyond small-scale agricultural production are available to local residents, and circular migration to more urbanized areas has characterized the northern districts for the past several generations. In this sense, the regional dynamic is one that is prevalent worldwide today: in terms of development, peripheries are treated as an afterthought, with few economic resources and little attention devoted to the quality of the built environment. Although

Human labor and social capital are at the heart of creating architecture.

The METI School and other projects realized in the village of Rudrapur, Bangladesh, demonstrate how local materials and human capacity can be maximized for sustainable building.

many structures in Northern Bangladesh are still erected using traditional techniques, wherever savings allow, people turn to imported materials and processes, such as concrete frames infilled with fired clay bricks. Not only is this ill-suited to the tropical savannah climate, it also results in a draining of local capital into the pockets of multinational corporations and precludes investment in the community. Moreover, this tendency also runs contrary to current goals of social sustainability as formulated by international development organizations such as the United Nations.

This chapter explores the failures of contemporary building practices, questioning the definition of sustainability and elaborating the environmental and social benefits of earth building. For what does exist in places like the peripheral areas of Bangladesh, indeed in abundance, is earth—that and the human capacity to build. It is this recognition of the inherent potentials of local Bangladeshi materials and social capital that underlies the conception of Anna Heringer's projects in Rudrapur, in the Dinajpur District of Rangpur. In terms of potential solutions for sustainable construction and for our future cities, such endeavors demonstrate how human labor has been maximized and technology minimized to suit the context of Bangladesh. This gradient between a reliance on social capital and an optimization of technological innovation is one of the greatest advantages of working with earth.

Building Bangladesh

A.H. There is an abundance of materials that nature provides for free. Although every farmer knows that an earth house is warmer in the winter and cooler in summer than a house made of bricks, earth does not look modern. Decades of colonialism and international development cooperation have promoted industrialized materials and accorded them a superior image. Development cooperation has predominantly followed a specific pattern: foreign organizations erect their structures, made of industrialized and imported materials, in the midst of vernacular buildings. These projects, also primarily planned from abroad, do not typically incorporate endogenous potentials or value local building traditions.

When I first began conceiving the Modern Education and Training Institute (METI) School, I wanted to build in exactly the opposite way: mud instead of bricks and concrete, bamboo instead of steel. Did my clients jump for joy when I proposed this? Not really! Earth and bamboo were perceived as the materials of the poor. But, the potential for job creation for local craftsmen and unskilled laborers, as well as the positive environmental impact of the materials, spoke in favor of implementing a mud-and-bamboo construction. The fact that local building techniques would be improved through the technical innovation and the skills-training the new building would bring were further pluses for this approach.

Admittedly, one of the most convincing factors in the decision was that I promised to raise the funding for the building. But in the end, it was the trust that the executive director of my NGO client Dipshikha, Paul Cherwa Tigga, had in me personally, after eight years of close collaboration and proven empathy for the country, which finally decided the matter. When I am asked if the idea for the METI School was "imposed," in the sense of development cooperation, I am not entirely sure. But my fundamental approach to any project since has been to maximize the available local materials, utilize local energy resources (especially people), and select the correct mix of local and global know-how. In particular, knowledge should not remain limited to a place, but rather function as an open-source resource to which anyone on the planet should have access. So any context can draw from global resources and apply them to their local condition.

During the construction of the METI School, I lived in the village of Rudrapur and often accompanied the workers to the market at the end of the day. I directly experienced how they spent the salary they had earned on the site. They typically bought vegetables from their neighbors, got their bicycle repaired in the local workshop, went to the barber, or ordered a new shirt from the tailor. Because the vast majority of the construction budget was spent on craftsmanship, the school was so much more than just a building: it was a catalyst for local development. This is what I remain most happy about. If I had designed the school in con-

The building culture in Rudrapur relied on available materials and resources.

crete and steel, this money would have been exported instead of invested in those families. After this experience, my mantra was no longer "the cheaper the better" or a low cost at any price. Instead it became "cui bono"? Who benefits? This question contains the true power of architecture and building. With all the budgets we control and our corresponding responsibility as designers, as clients, as developers, as NGOs, and as politicians, we must ensure that we construct a fair society as we construct its buildings.

Bamboo provided an appropriate solution to complement earth building techniques.

After I built the METI School, I interned as a construction worker on the building site of Martin Rauch's house in Vorarlberg, Austria. What really left an impression on me at the time was how technical the process was. There were so many tools, so much technical equipment, and so much expertise required, compared to building with earth in Bangladesh. In Bangladesh, so much was done by hand—practically our only tools were a spade and our water buffalos. Martin's building site was so loud, and everything moved so quickly despite having so few people on site! After overcoming my initial shock about the process, I was fascinated with the material. In particular, I connected with the ramming process through the act of compacting, and through retouching the finished products—sealing the gaps between elements or touching up damaged places, which is done by hand. From the windows to the walls, everything in earth is of the highest and most modern quality, both physically and architecturally.

Concrete: The Elephant in the Room

The production of cement and concrete uses more resources than any other industry on the planet. Recent reports originating from the private sector estimate that 8 percent of total global greenhouse-gas emissions come from concrete—and that it is the second-most-consumed substance on earth after water.[1] A report by the Royal Institute of International Affairs notes: "To bring the cement sector in line with the Paris Agreement on climate change, its annual emissions will need to fall by at least 16 per cent by 2030."[2] Direct emissions occur through calcination, when limestone is heated and breaks down into calcium oxide and carbon dioxide (accounting for 50 percent of total concrete industry emissions); indirectly, emissions occur when fossil fuels are used to heat the kiln (40 percent); and energy is also used for electricity to run plants and for transport (5 to 10 percent). Moreover, this still excludes the effects of aggregate extraction, running mixing plants, or water usage. In total, this process produces approximately 3.3 billion tons of carbon dioxide per year—over three times more carbon dioxide annually than the sum total of all global emissions related to airplane travel.[3] Every ton of cement results in 800 kilograms of carbon dioxide emissions, primarily because the clinker must be heated to 1,800 degrees Celsius. On a building scale, this means each truckload of cement utilized for construction requires 22,000 tons of carbon dioxide to produce.[4]

Even if concrete were able to be fully recycled, it still requires finite resources—for example, sand and gravel—to produce more. If one were to build a wall along the equator with all the sand and gravel mined each and every year to produce concrete, it would be 27 meters high.[5] Thus, regardless of whether or not concrete can be branded as "green," or elements or components of it can be recycled, its production and distribution require an energy baseline that means it can never become truly sustainable. Although cement-based materials are vital for structural design in densely urban as well as earthquake-prone contexts, the reality is that their use remains disproportionately greater than is structurally or seismically necessary.

Building with earth and building with concrete are not mutually exclusive. The philosophy we advocate in our projects and in this book is simply to utilize as little cement as possible. Comparing the comprehensive footprints of production for concrete and rammed earth support this assertion. Such footprints are referred to by economists in terms of externalities, namely the benefits or damages inflicted on a neutral third party during the production or consumption of goods or a service.[6] Because building materials are evaluated according to such different parameters, it is difficult to cross-compare them, but, all things considered, the externalities of earth are largely positive while those of cement-based materials are almost entirely negative.

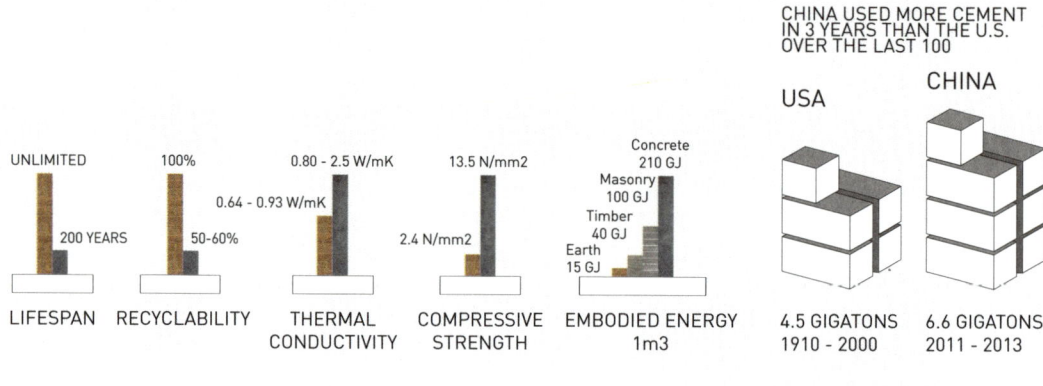

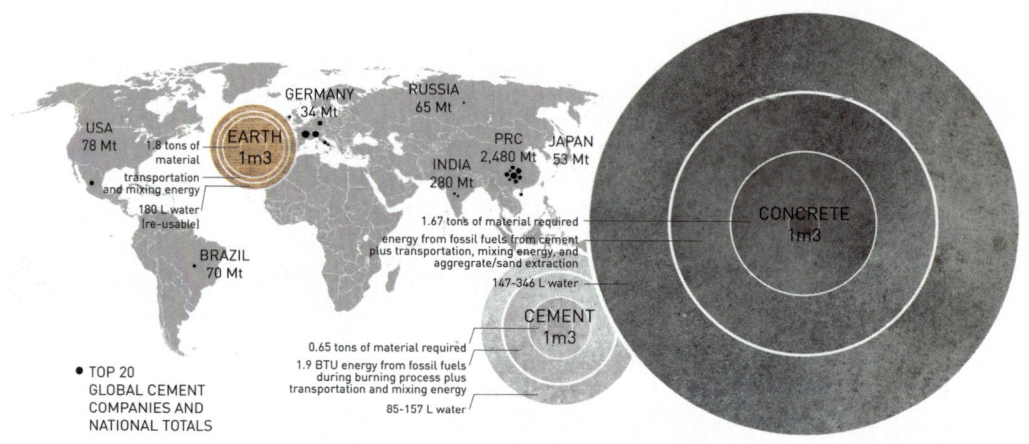

Designs must be imagined as a ripple that impacts seven billion people. Eight percent of global greenhouse gas emissions currently come from concrete—what is the true cost of using so much of it? Illustration: Lindsay Blair Howe.

To elaborate: mineral resources are finite. Both concrete and rammed earth include gravel and sand, and both require immense amounts of energy to extract from the ground, whereas this expenditure is significantly smaller in the case of earth. However, these calculations further diverge in that the production of the cement prerequisite for concrete consumes significantly more resources through the aforementioned burning process. There are also fundamental differences in gray energy. If an earth building requires 1.8 tons of material—as was the case with Haus Rauch, for example—this necessitates

180 liters of water, energy for excavating the earth from the site, and energy for obtaining, transporting, and mixing any additional materials such as gravel.[7] A project of the same volume executed with concrete would require 1.67 tons of material, between 147 to 347 liters of water, additional energy for excavation and transporting the unused earth from digging the foundations away, and even more energy for obtaining, transporting, and mixing the cement-based concrete and its aggregates. In addition, 1.9 British Thermal Units (BTUs)[8] of nonrenewable energy are needed to fire the amount of cement for this mixture, as well as a further 85 to 157 liters of water.[9] And, the water for the production of concrete is not gray water that can be recycled and reused, as it is with rammed earth: it contains toxic chemicals.

Moreover, in the case of concrete, significant economic and environmental costs are accrued due to building climate control and the maintenance throughout a building's life cycle. Climate control, particularly heating and cooling, contributes to energy use, as well as causing environmental damage. With air-conditioning, this is primarily because of noxious refrigerants and electricity use. Recent studies have indicated that the estimated 1.6 billion new air conditioners that will be installed by 2050 in countries like Mexico, Brazil, and India will significantly impact the ozone layer and contribute to climate change—which, paradoxically, will encourage the purchase of even more air conditioners.[10] As economists Lucas Davis and Paul Gertler describe, not just the increased demand for electricity for these units will be problematic, requiring trillions of dollars in power generation and transmission infrastructure, but they will likely lead to shortages and price spikes in services.[11] "In addition," notes climate scientist Nihar Shar of the Lawrence Berkeley National Laboratory, "most electricity worldwide continues to be generated using fossil fuels, so this growth in air conditioning means billions of tons of increased carbon dioxide emissions."[12]

An Illusion of Permanence

L.B.H. The speed of contemporary urbanization increases the negative externalities of concrete astronomically, impacting not only the structure of space but also the norms of building cultures. In pursuit of alleged modernity and permanence, the planet becomes a macrocosm of Paul Ricœur's "jettisoning of the cultural past," described by Kenneth Frampton in his critique of an architecture dominated by universalism and technology.[13] In a globalized chain of construction processes, local inflections and social values are suppressed, while the true costs of building with concrete are also substantially underestimated. The paradox, Ricœur notes, is that "the phenomenon of universalization, while being an advancement of mankind, at the same time constitutes a sort of subtle destruction."[14]

Even if one disregards the high costs, negative externalities, and "cultural jettisoning" of designing with universalized, fossil-fuel-based materials, concrete buildings remain far removed from the permanence modernism professed. At the Shenzhen Bi-City Biennale in 2015, I supervised our contribution to an exhibition entitled Re-living the City, which aimed to envision how our future cities might appear if they were constructed primarily in rammed earth rather than concrete. To provide visitors with a tangible representation of rammed earth, I planned the construction of a 1:1-scale mock-up of a small living space on the second floor of the exhibition space. The building had previously served as grain storage for a mill, able to carry the weight of sacks of wheat stacked over five floors to the height of the nearly 4-meter-high ceilings. Our team carefully adhered to all of the original static regulations for the building, which were set at 2,000 kilograms

A custom crane was developed to lift prefabricated panels into place for the Shenzhen Re-living the City Architecture and Urbanism Biennale Exhibition (2015).

Leo Steiger oversaw the prefabrication process for the collaborative project developed by the ETH Zurich, Xi'an University, and Lehm Ton Erde GmbH.

Since the compressive strength of the Shenzhen Biennale's concrete building could not be verified, instead of building an enclosed space as originally planned, a "corner" was constructed and supplemented with panels about earth building.

per square meter, and meticulously calculated point and live loads to design the installation. A custom-fabricated crane was even engineered by our project partner at Xi'an University, Professor Mu Jun, so we could ram prefabricated earthen elements and set them in place directly in the space to show the full scope of current technological innovation.

However, midway into the construction process, a team of consultant civil engineers for the biennale organizers ordered an immediate freeze; they were uncertain that the numbers we had been given to calculate the loads with were accurate. They did not want to assume liability for the structure's concrete. Since it had been built in the 1980s, the engineers explained, they did not have any information on the quality of the sand that had been used in the mixture, making it impossible to completely verify the concrete's compressive strength. "Who knows if the concrete is reliable today?" they said. After several tense days of back-and-forth, we arrived at a solution, instead constructing just half of the originally planned rammed earth room and enclosing the living space with light wooden panels. These panels displayed information about cutting-edge projects built with earth—and the negative externalities of concrete as a global industrial complex with a much higher impact on the environment than that of earth.

One of the most memorable results of this exhibition was how much the earthen walls spoke to people—not just to the biennale's participants and visitors, but also to the building's installation and cleaning crews. I often arrived at the construction site in the morning to see someone running their fingers along the walls; they were enthralled, they told me through intermediaries, with how beautifully modern the material they knew so well from their rural villages could appear.

No other material I have encountered is simultaneously so authentic and so elegant, so adaptable and sustainable, be it in the context of an extended urban region like Shenzhen or the bush of Botswana. There is no reason to jettison our oldest building materials in the name of permanence or modernity—on the contrary, we can also use contemporary technologies to realize their full potential for specific cultures and values. Juxtaposed in this way, it seems clear that the use of concrete should be minimized and earth be upscaled to build our future cities.

A Catalyst for Labor and Technology

In the quest to increase sustainability, both academic research and private-sector initiatives alike are beginning to investigate the impact of construction on the planet and its inhabitants. In this process, the fusion of ancient, vernacular earth building techniques with modern requirements is one of many potential solutions so urgently needed to combat the negative externalities of our current construction industry. If earth can match the appropriate cultural and contextual conditions of each project with local materials as well as local participation, this allows building to become a process rather than a product—or beyond that even a *catalyst*, reframing sustainable building while engendering socially just development.

There is an unmistakable dominance of mechanically produced materials and highly technical processes in contemporary architecture—backed by vast sums of capital investment. Earthen architecture can certainly profit from technical innovation. Historically, it has sufficed to have just a few experienced technical experts to oversee an earth building site; the physical act of construction can be executed by untrained laborers. This emphasis on building by means of social capital has faded away from common practice, particularly in highly urbanized and industrialized contexts. However, the degree to which technology is a part of the building process can be matched to the requirements of each unique culture and context in earth building, with construction methods ranging from the fully manual to the completely industrialized and prefabricated. The key point is that, in theory, knowledge of how to conduct the entire chain of production can be transferred to the beneficiaries of the intended project when constructing with earth. This kind of "fairness" is a characteristic seldom exhibited by building materials and construction processes tied to global cycles of profit and loss.

As previously alluded to, a specific kind of earth building suited to the cultural context can also act as a catalyst for social development. When considering the issue of social impact, we inevitably return to the questions: Who profits? And does the money invested in construction flow back to the project's beneficiaries? We can imagine this as a gradient between projects which are fully manually executed with human labor and those which rely on technology and mechanization. Each building culture requires a specific balance along this gradient, corresponding to available resources, the cost of skilled and unskilled labor, and aesthetic standards, as exemplified by the projects discussed in this book. Either way, when building with earth, the goal should be to involve people to the greatest degree possible. Corresponding to this gradient, when projects are executed directly by those who will later occupy them, people can learn the skills to maintain these structures as well as how to produce further iterations of the processes involved. If a high level of technology is used—for example, in highly urbanized contexts—these occupants themselves may be more removed from the process of construction. Nevertheless, involving people in the process, as can be done with earth, inherently has the potential to disrupt—and positively impact—our current building practices.

If sustainability means living in harmony with the natural environment and society, and mitigating the impact of global capitalism to the fullest extent possible, then the METI School is like a microcosm of these principles:

> All too often, aspirations towards modernity in developing countries have malign economic and cultural effects where construction is concerned. Traditional materials and techniques are abandoned in favor of the import of expensive and sometimes energy-inefficient materials and products, benefiting only manufacturers in more advanced economies. The outcome can at worst be the imposition of alien buildings, forms and materials which do not last long and are difficult to maintain. Their only merit is to look new for a time.
>
> [The METI School], this joyful project, in a poor rural area of Bangladesh (said to be the world's most densely populated country), shows that new and refreshing local identity can be achieved by exploiting the immediate and the readily available.[15]

The METI School in Rudrapur is a paradigmatic example of how appropriate construction can become a catalyst for further socioeconomic development. As opposed to projects—in particular those in the name of international development—that emphasize imported and expensive materials, not only did the METI School involve a transfer of skills and the retention of capital within local society, but the act of building itself engendered multiple long-term initiatives to increase the economic independence of the community. As a catalyst, this investment in social capital represents a best-practice example of how development cooperation can succeed—grounded in a thorough understanding of the local building culture and socioeconomic structures.

The metric for success or failure of projects executed for development and cooperation should therefore be threefold: (1) Is the construction material appropriate? (2) Is the outcome both a product *and* a process? (3) Is the project a catalyst?

Including local labor, particularly women, in the construction processes in Rudrapur ensured that profits remained within the community.

Architecture became a catalyst for development, as people involved in the Rudrapur projects were able to utilize their building knowledge for further projects and reinvest their earnings into other small business initiatives.

When materials are upscaled and produced in an industrial fashion, there will always be a trade-off between the number of people that can be engaged in the building process and the level of technical standards that can be achieved. This is why the scalability of earth as a building material remains relevant for almost any building context. Particularly in our interdependent world, earth is uniquely positioned to embody socially conscious principles of construction, in which the local stands to benefit from the global. There is always a connection between the materials with which we choose to build and the responsibility all of us share toward each other and the planet.

1   Johanna Lehne and Felix Preston, *Making Concrete Change: Innovation in Low-Carbon Cement and Concrete*, Chatham House Report, Royal Institute of International Affairs: Energy, Environment and Resources Department, June 2018, v.
2   Ibid.
3   Judith Schneider, "Zement—der heimliche Klimakiller," *Planet-E*, ZDF (first broadcast May 5, 2018), https://www.youtube.com/watch?v=hEx5XshkFIw&ab_channel=UpscalingEarth
4   René Ammann, e-mail supplement to *World Architects eMagazine*, 05/18 (January 30, 2018).
5   Ibid.
6   See Elinor Ostrom, *Governing the Commons: The Evolution of Institutions for Collective Action* (Cambridge: Cambridge University Press, 1990).
7   Martin Rauch, personal interview by Lindsay Blair Howe, November 3, 2015.

8   One BTU is the amount of heat needed to raise the temperature of one pound of water by one degree Fahrenheit. Its equivalent in the metric system is the calorie, which corresponds to heating one gram of water by one degree Celsius. One BTU is also equal to 1,055 joules of energy. See G. Woledge, "History of the British Thermal Unit," *Nature*, 49, no. 3787 (1949), p. 613.
9   Sean Xun, "The Mineral Industry of China," *U.S. Geological Survey Minerals Yearbook—2014*, U.S. Department of the Interior (2017), sections 8.1–8.4 and 8.8.
10 Nihar Shah, as cited in interview with Jeremy Hobson, "World on Pace to Install 700 Million More Air Conditioners by 2030," *Here & Now* (Boston: WBUR 90.9, Boston's NPR News Station, 2016), http://www.wbur.org/hereandnow/2016/06/02/world-air-conditioners (accessed September 8, 2018).
11 Lucas W. Davis and Paul J. Gertler, "Contribution of Air Conditioning Adoption to Future Energy Use under Global Warming," *Proceedings of the National Academy of Sciences of the United States of America*, 112, no. 19 (2015), pp. 5962–7, here p. 5962.
12 Shah, "700 Million More Air Conditioners" (see note 10).
13 Paul Ricoeur, as cited in Kenneth Frampton, "Towards a Critical Regionalism: Six Points for an Architectural Resistance," in Hal Foster (ed.), *The Anti-aesthetic: Essays on Postmodern Culture* (Port Townsen: Bay Press, 1983), pp. 16–30, here p. 16.
14 Ibid.
15 Paul Finch, "Earth Works: Handmade School, Rudrapur, Bangladesh," *Architectural Review*, 220, no. 1318 (2006), pp. 40–43.

Material

Imagine the procedural evolution of building a tunnel. Long ago, when one wanted to excavate through a mountain, the only tools available were a chisel and a hammer. Based on empirical knowledge and experience, the most favorable location was determined and the chipping away began: an excruciating amount of labor paired with the simplest of technological approaches. As we progressed to the invention of dynamite, the process of tunnel building fundamentally changed. Today, machines over 100 meters long are capable of drilling a tunnel from start to finish. One ramification of this transition—from hand-hewn projects, which often had significant limitations in regard to scale and feasibility, to machine-based approaches—is a significant reduction in the amount of manpower required.

Earth as a building material has the potential to operate across this entire gradient from high-labor to high-technology approaches, with a plethora of combinations in between. Two of the primary and interconnected reasons it has nevertheless receded from collective architectural practices are that the Industrial Revolution made mass-produced materials cheaper and more accessible and that, parallel to this process, earth became stigmatized as regressive, even becoming a symbol of poverty. This chapter first examines

A high-labor approach to ramming earth in Addis Ababa, Ethiopia.

A low-labor, technologically intensive method automating the fabrication of earthen elements in Darmstadt, Germany.

the meaning of earth as a building material, in particular the roots of rammed earth and the trajectory of its use. It explicates the two key reasons for its reduced use in industrialized contexts and for its renewed appeal today. Then, it delves into the material properties and benefits of rammed earth. It defines the process of creating rammed earth, as well as groundbreaking current innovations in the prefabrication of earthen components that can *upscale* the material for potential mass production.

The Image of Earth

M.R. Josef Frank, a pioneer of the Vienna School and anti-ideologue of the modern era, declared earth the most elemental building material of humankind. From this perspective, earth is not a building material but rather a *Weltanschauung*.[1] Historically, earth was connected to the idea of necessity, of creating shelter from the most widely available material for the greatest number of people. However, unlike our analogy with the tunnel, there is no direct path between the early use of earth as a handcrafted building material and later technological advances.

There have also been long periods of silence along this path—primarily due to the image of earth worldwide. Colonization in the 1800s began to recast the image of earthen architecture as something foreign, archaic, and even primitive. In many colonialized countries, the same natural building material had been used across building typologies, whether rich or poor, private or public. The primary differences were in size and in the ornamentation or furnishings of the space. The kasbahs of Morocco or earthen towers of Yemen and Saudi Arabia are examples of this kind of logic embedded in building practices. But through colonization, European building culture, with its hierarchies and technologies, was exported along with the industrialized materials themselves.

In this way, long before global sales of concrete commenced, industrialized nations began to shape the image of what modern building should be in foreign countries. Bricks and brickmaking technology were spread around the world by ship, for example, reducing the image of earth building in these far-flung places as well. During project work in England, a brick producer once told me that colonial cargo ships were often filled with high-quality fired bricks and exported abroad. This was necessary because, at the time, the English were primarily importing, and the ships traveling afar were largely empty, requiring more weight to simulate their ballast and cargo. The bricks were then unloaded at their port of arrival and exchanged for further goods, or used to construct the first structures for foreign residences or businesses. Later, once brick was established as a building material, it became a part of the urbanization process; brickmaking machines and technical expertise were exported too.

Early Experimentation with Rammed Earth

M.R. Rammed earth can be defined as an earth mixture including clay, sand, and gravel, which is filled into formwork and compacted layer by layer to form a contiguous whole. Earth was historically used to create a wide range of structures, from huts to palaces. One of the earliest attempts at establishing rammed earth as a building practice occurred in the 1700s, when experiments with earthen architecture were conducted by architect François Cointeraux prior to the French Revolution.[2] Cointeraux is credited with having "discovered" rammed earth, or what he referred to as *pisé de terre*, in the region surrounding Lyon.[3] Paralleling the challenges of today, he saw earth as an opportunity for sustainability, not only in terms of resources but also social practice, driven by a belief that it could benefit both the wealthy and the increasing number of underprivileged in France.

Historically, crises have often been a driver of innovation and an opportunity for change. The wars and social restructuring of Europe in the 1700s, for example, led to significant innovations in the building culture of the continent. In 1764, Frederick the Great introduced earth building through an ordinance in East and West Prussia, which at the time suffered a dearth in the supply of timber and stone.[4] Experienced technical experts in earth building

Material

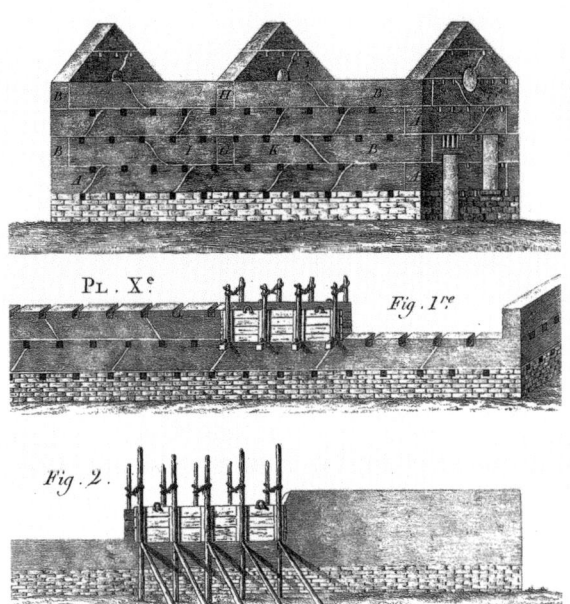

Elevations of a rammed earth structure and the ramming process, by François Cointeraux.

from what is now Central Germany were employed to teach their craft to the Prussian population. The Prussian state also constructed larger buildings using earthen techniques, bringing a discussion about this kind of building culture into public discourse. While there are no historical records of how many structures were built, the fact that so many constructions from this period remain standing today speaks to the effectiveness and impact of Frederick the Great's decree.

The vernacular buildings of this era were simple massive constructions, primarily so to prevent fires from spreading. Whether of stone, fired brick, or simple adobe bricks, they were typically covered with some form of plaster and had the same exterior appearance. Sun-dried adobe bricks were used very frequently. Simple and inexpensive to produce, they merely required adequate time to dry to comprise a relatively high-quality building material.[5] Such bricks were often referred to as *Luftsteine* (air stones) or *Luftziegel* (air bricks) in German. They competed directly with the more expensive, pit-fired clay bricks, the latter also being one of the main reasons for the large-scale deforestation to provide the wood needed to burn in their production, along with other industrial processes. Since brick, and indeed natural stone—which was even more expensive due to the labor and transportation costs it involved—were unaffordable for a majority of the population, some form of earth construction was integrated into most vernacular structures at the time.

Rammed earth was also in use; publications were already in circulation about improving formwork systems and optimizing the correct tools to use for the ramming process.[6] The first known formal publication on refining earth building, or *pisé*, had in fact already been printed in 1772 in France.[7] What, however, could have represented the onset of innovation was soon quashed through the onset of the Industrial Revolution. Through industrialization, earth huts no longer befitted the processes of modernization, and because they could not be mass-produced they were certainly not a part of the emerging systems of capital accumulation. Regional networks by rail and global networks by sea made mass-produced building materials significantly less expensive to transport, meaning that they could be produced and sold in burgeoning worldwide supply chains. Finally, earth was deemed an inadequate means to define the new image of the emerging bourgeoisie. Earth building began to be plagued by stereotypes and lacked investment to advance its development, causing it to fade into disuse.

Rammed Earth: Naturally Resilient

Erosion and structural stability are two of the most common concerns cited by architects when expressing apprehensions about designing with earth, so the ability to test and prove consistent material properties is central to increasing the use of earth in contemporary building practices. One current trend contributing—at least ostensibly—to the promotion of earth as a building material is *stabilization*. Stabilizing earth refers to supplementing the natural earth mixture with chemical additives, such as cement. Commonly,

Material

a 5–10 percent cement solution is added to the earth mixture, assuaging fears of material erosion due to weathering or lack of adequate compressive strength. Many rammed earth projects by renowned architects have been executed in this fashion for example, the works of Francis Kéré in Burkina Faso, Rick Joy in the United States, or Luigi Rosselli in Australia. These projects contain as much as 10 percent cement mixtures—nearly as high a ratio as the standard 12 percent cement mixture in concrete. Not only is stabilization unnecessary, it actually destroys the two most valuable physical properties of the material earth: its ability to exchange moisture and its full recyclability.

There are four factors at work here. Firstly, the retention of water vapor and "trapped" humidity are often cited as reasons to avoid the thick, load-bearing kind of construction that rammed earth in particular embodies. However, precisely the opposite is true: absorbing and expelling moisture is one of its most remarkable properties. Because untreated rammed earth can still breathe, the building and its occupants can exchange moisture, and excess condensation is transmitted out of the wall through capillary action.[8] This hygroscopic characteristic results in a constant room temperature and humidity, regardless of the season. In the few studies that have been conducted to date, such as with Haus Rauch and in our ETH Zurich design-build semester project for housing and a community center in Tanzania, these properties have been shown to mean that significantly fewer resources are required for long-term operation and maintenance—all of which result in lower impact and lower costs. These properties are practically impossible to reverse engineer.

Secondly, earth is water-soluble, indeed making it vulnerable to weathering and environmental conditions. However, this fact is also an astonishing resource. Instead of trying to artificially compensate for this deterioration, rammed earth construction should follow the principle of *calculated erosion*.

One of the most beneficial properties of building with earth is that—if it is not stabilized with chemical-based additives—it can be recycled infinitely or folded back into the ground. Schematic drawings: CRAterre and Studio Anna Heringer.

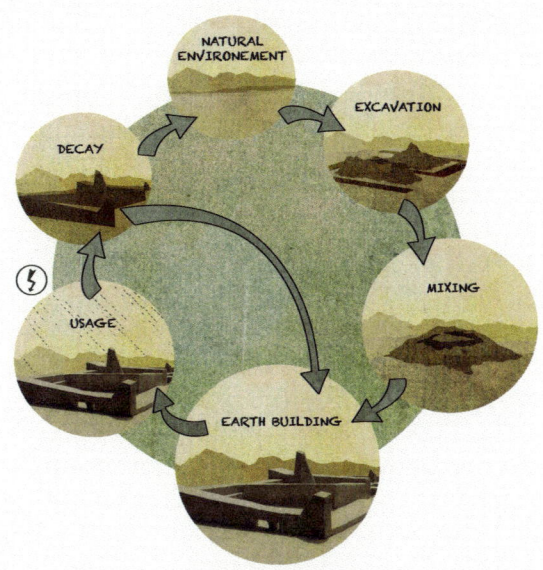

Calculated erosion requires that the walls of a structure are initially built 2 or 3 centimeters thicker than would have otherwise been planned. As water runoff begins to weather the façade, protruding stones break up the flows of water from further permeating the walls and eroding clay from the mixture. The clay particles in the mixture also naturally expand in response to increased moisture, contributing to the cessation of weathering. To support this process, speed breakers should be planned into the façade—horizontal strips of a protruding material, or trass lime flush with the walls, inserted at selected intervals.at selected intervals. Countless projects relying on this system worldwide have proven that, after the initial attrition of several centimeters, the façade ceases to recede under regular weather conditions. As long as the quality of the earth mixture is sufficient, and it is compacted correctly, even earthen buildings with flat roofs can withstand weathering if they are built taking calculated erosion into account.

Thirdly, chemical-based additives significantly reduce the ability to recycle earth. If nothing is added to an earthen building, when the structure is no longer required its component parts can be removed, and it can simply be folded back into the ground to decompose or be reused for new earthen buildings. If substances such as cement are added, the material can perhaps be used for further rounds of construction, but this process entails continual degradation and eventual disuse. In sum, it can never be fully recycled like untreated earth.

The final factor is practicality. In choosing to design with the material earth as found rather than altering it with additives, both its most beneficial properties as well as its unique localized characteristics can be retained. Some regions of the world have a high gravel content in their earth, making rammed earth a natural choice for building. Others, like Bangladesh, have little gravel but have an abundance of straw, making cob building an appropriate technique. Each means of construction results in its own aesthetic, its own set of rules that suit its climate and meet its occupants' sociocultural requirements for comfort.

Our approach as designers is to take earth's inherent parameters—the characteristics of the local climate and the local earth mixture—very seriously. These factors challenge our creative impulses and make each product authentic, while also embodying a common-sense approach to architecture and design.

The Potential of Prefabrication

The unique potential of rammed earth as a stable, durable, and healthy building material is suited to most climatic contexts and is currently contributing to a transformation of the image of earth. Constructing long-lasting, sustainable buildings with nothing more than formwork, compacting layer after layer of earth mixtures by hand with tampers, can yield designs of the highest architectural quality. However, such an approach is not realistic for many industrialized parts of the world, where labor is expensive. In such contexts, prefabrication is more appropriate, representing the opposite end of the gradient between labor and technology: the ability to deliver component rammed earth elements.

There are two means of producing rammed earth elements such as walls: creating them in situ or prefabricating them. In either case, the first step in production is to install formwork; for example, the same sort of formwork that can be used for pouring concrete. Prefabricated rammed earth elements are typically executed in formwork 50–80 meters long and 1.3 meters high and

Machine conceived by Lehm Ton Erde GmbH to prefabricate with a mechanized ramming process.

The material mixture is distributed into the formwork and then rammed by the machine.

located in a warehouse so that the materials can be produced regardless of the site schedule or weather conditions. One of the two formwork walls is fixed in place and the second is movable, such that the width of the wall can be adjusted for each project and the elements easily removed from this shell. When ramming with a machine, it is affixed to the immovable side. It can robotically distribute the material into the formwork as well as tamper the poured material.

Material

The ramming machine pours a material mixture in 12–15 centimeter increments into the formwork; the particles of this mixture must be no larger than 3.2 centimeters. When it is compacted, the layer will reduce to 6–8 centimeters. Once ramming is completed and the adjustable wall removed, the entire length of the prefabricated wall is then cut into the required component parts. The size is most commonly determined by the maximum weight a crane can carry when lifting the elements into place on the building site; this relative size is in turn determined by the intention to leave the continuous pattern of the earth as intact as possible. In this sense, the process mirrors the aesthetic of in situ rammed earth, achieved by setting the elements into place with an earthen form of mortar that hides the seams of the components themselves. The elements are also *retouched* by hand with the same mortar substance to create a completely seamless finished surface. A wall or wall element executed in this way requires four to six weeks to dry in the warehouse, after which it will have reached its full load-bearing capacity.

The prefabrication process not only optimizes production and the construction process; it also allows for material consistency and higher-quality output, which are particularly important for achieving industrialized norms and standards. With earth, the overall product is determined by its contextually unique elements: the clay utilized, the sand and gravel added to the earth to form the mixture, the moisture level of the mixture during ramming, the stability of climatic conditions during the production process, and the con-

Earthen elements are stored in a warehouse until they reach their full compressive strength and material stability by naturally drying.

Modular elements (here, cavity walls with integrated insulation) can be fully produced in advance and then set into place according to the requirements of the building site schedule.

sistency of the ramming itself. All of these aspects have a direct impact on the rammed earth's compressive strength, load-bearing capacities, thermal properties, moisture absorption ratio, and fire rating. They can be carefully controlled and tested in a laboratory setting through prefabrication, as is the case for concrete or other standardized, industrialized materials.

Innovation through Building

M.R. Today, confronted with crises the scale of which humankind has never known, the immense power of earth is once again urgently required. A renaissance in rammed earth, in particular, is beginning to blossom across the world, especially on the European continent. It provides a taste of how much more advanced this building process might have been were it to have enjoyed the similar decades of innovation that easily commodified materials such as concrete have undergone. Nevertheless, the very fact that earth is reasserting itself, and this despite its lack of a powerful lobby or major source of funding, demonstrates that it still has the potential to fundamentally reframe what it means to create sustainable architecture. The vital question, therefore, is: How we can address these deficits while successfully and appropriately building with earth, meeting both modern standards of living as well as the challenges of an ever-more technological architectural discourse?

Contemporary rammed earth building has consistently been associated with design and technical innovation. The first major prefabricated project executed in rammed earth by Lehm Ton Erde, my company in the Vorarlberg region of Austria, was for the Gugler Printing House near St. Pölten. The prefabricated rammed-earth components in this project were conceived as a hypocaust: a chamber in which warm air is circulated to act as a heating system. Innovation has primarily functioned like this, as "research-by-design," in which the development of prefabricated components has been conducted through our projects. By 2007, we were able to produce multiple components within a single line of formwork. The first large-scale project in which

The Gugler Printing House (1998–1999) in Pielach, Austria, was planned with architects Ablinger, Vedral & Partners and contained 160 prefabricated earthen elements.

both the production and material distribution occurred by machine was in 2012 for the Ricola Kräuterzentrum in Laufen, Switzerland. We invented a machine that could distribute and also ram the mixture into the formwork for the Swiss Ornithological Institute in 2014 in Sempach. Finally, in 2016, we produced the first rammed earth components with integrated insulation systems for the Alnatura Arbeitswelt project in Darmstadt, Germany.

Prefabricated ramming is essential to realizing the full potential of earth as a building material. Earth is primarily used in non-load-bearing contexts today, when it is in fact perfectly capable of acting as both the load-bearing and insulating element in a building façade. Research into prefabricating load-bearing, exterior cavity walls with built-in insulation has been conducted by Lehm Ton Erde for the past twenty years, and we are currently expanding the scope of our research to encompass the prefabrication of elements such as columns, girders, and brackets. This research is simultaneously producing new forms of rammed earth elements, including testing the properties of their building physics and life cycles. Finally, we are currently developing standardized connecting elements to join prefabricated rammed earth and other building components, such as ceiling and floor slabs, doors and windows, and also to act as integrated conduits for piping and wiring. Creating such standardized elements is essential to the process of upscaling earth into a viable building material, particularly for highly industrialized contexts.

Students of Professor Annette Spiro and Lecturer Gian Salis at the ETH Zurich designed and prefabricated elements to create the first-ever rammed earth vault, working in close collaboration with Lehm Ton Erde GmbH.

Six elements comprising two separate components and spanned by vaults were lifted into place on their site on the ETH Zurich Hönggerberg campus, with a hexagonal keystone, and then their joints were retouched to create a seamless surface.

But the elevation of earth as a building material does not just occur through projects in which components become ever more technically complex. Earthen architecture requires its own formal language. In 2012, a partnership with Annette Spiro and Gian Salis at the ETH Zurich Department of Architecture attempted to combine prefabrication and form-finding approaches. In an elective course, students were presented with an unparalleled challenge: design the world's first cupola with prefabricated, unstabilized earthen-component parts. The 5-meter-high design that resulted from this seminar comprised six arches supporting five dome-like structures. These parts were lifted into place with cranes and fused together with an earth-lime mixture that acts like mortar between bricks. While pure unstabilized earth

Material

Minimal concrete foundations provide a stable base for the cupola. It is protected from weather by metal roofing.

must indeed function as a compression-only structure, the cupola proved that innovative design approaches and contemporary technological tools have the capacity not just to elevate a building material but to also expand our notions of how we can create an architectural language and architectonic expression for earth.

1   Bruno Maldoner and Wilhelm Schmid, "Zum traditionellen Lehmbau in Österreich: Eine Annäherung," *Denkmalpflege in Niederösterreich*, Vol. 39: *Lehm und Ziegel*, pp. 6–10. (St. Pölten: Amt der NÖ Landesregierung Abteilung Kultur und Wissenschaft, 2007).
2   For a discussion of earthen architecture in the Swiss and European historical contexts, see Roger Boltshauser, Cyril Veillon, and Nadja Maillard (eds.), *Pisé – Stampflehm: Tradition und Potential* (Zurich: Triest Verlag, 2018).
3   François Cointeraux, *École d'architecture rurale, ou Leçons par lesquelles on apprendra soi-même à bâtir solidement les maisons de plusieurs étages, avec la terre seule ou autres matériaux les plus communs et du plus vil prix* (Paris: l'Auteur, 1790).
4   See Hildegard Erhard, *Kleine Geschichte der Lehmarchitektur in Deutschland*, in Jean Dethier (ed.), *Lehmarchitektur: Die Zukunft einer vergessenen Bautradition* (Munich: Prestel-Verlag, 1982), pp. 200–209.
5   David Gilly, *Handbuch der Landbaukunst: Kupfersammlung zum Handbuch der Landbaukunst* (Charleston: Nabu Press, 2014 [originally 1818]).
6   See, for instance, Wilhelm Jacob Wimpf, *Der Pisébau oder die vollständige Anweisung äusserst wohlfeile, dauerhafte, warme und feuerfeste Wohnungen aus blosser gestampfter Erde, zu erbauen* (Heilbronn: Classische Buchhandlung, 1841).
7   See Clough Williams-Ellis and J. and E. Eastwick-Field, *Building in Cob, Pisé and Stabilized Earth* (London: 1947 [originally 1919]), pp. 103–12.
8   Marco Sauer (ed.), *Martin Rauch: Refined Earth—Construction & Design with Rammed Earth* (Munich: Detail Verlag, 2016), pp. 69, 74–77. See also Ulrich Röhlen and Christof Ziegert, *Lehmbau-Praxis: Planung und Ausführung*, 2nd ed. (Berlin: Beuth Verlag, 2014); Günter Zur Nieden and Christof Ziegert, *Neue Lehm-Häuser international: Projektbeispiele, Konstruktion, Details* (Berlin: Bauwerk Verlag, 2002).

Process

In the pursuit of upscaling earthen architecture, this chapter explores a range of projects by Anna Heringer and Martin Rauch that reflect different degrees of labor and technology. What ties all of their projects together, whether individually or working in collaboration, is their cumulative nature: in order to innovate, each work builds on the knowledge amassed through the projects that have come before. They reflect not just the upscaling of earth as a material—an improvement in its quality and execution—but as an increasingly optimized process, attempting to benefit the most people possible with the fewest nonrenewable resources feasible.

Our conception of sustainable building, as embodied by the projects and the teaching we conduct around the globe, is a building culture that seeks to utilize earth to its fullest extent while minimizing negative externalities; for instance, avoiding the use of materials like cement or processes like stabilization.

However, many design professionals, contractors, institutions, and governments remain highly skeptical of building with rammed earth—especially when the earth is load-bearing and not just a façade. First and foremost among skeptics are concerns about the performance of the material: How can it be standardized for mass production, and what is its ability to meet norms and codes? Convincing a wider audience requires well-documented flagship projects, in particular those that demonstrate an optimal balance between local labor and technical innovation.

The projects presented in this chapter demonstrate the trajectory of building with earth, as an accumulated body of knowledge. The investigations by both Heringer and Rauch began in under-resourced contexts, emerging from the basic impulse to create shelter with the mud surrounding us. These principles were then adapted for projects in Europe to prove that the material was just as relevant in urbanized contexts and that it could withstand the climate. Each project became a testament to the fact that building with earth had the capacity to be a modern way of creating a durable, beautiful architectonic object. And each endeavor also required winning the trust of clients and design professionals, to prove that earth was the best material and process for the project. After presenting a best-practice project that epitomizes earth as a *process*, this chapter chronicles the various forms of upscaling that projects involving Heringer and Rauch represent—a personal narrative about the insight derived from working with earth.

Ricola Kräuterzentrum

Years: 2012–2013
Location: Laufen, Switzerland
Architects: Herzog & de Meuron
Client: Ricola Ltd.
Details: prefabricated rammed earth walls non-load-bearing 1,240 m², 1,130 tons

Contemporary architectural details of the Ricola Kräuterzentrum (2012–2013) in Laufen, Switzerland.

M.R. The Ricola Kräuterzentrum, constructed by Lehm Ton Erde GmbH in collaboration with Herzog & de Meuron Architects, represents a paradigm shift in working with earth. This project is a culmination of our practical knowledge, technical innovation, and a close collaboration between designers and technical experts. Located just outside Basel in Switzerland, it is the first well-known example of using prefabricated earth parts on a large scale in a highly industrialized society. Earth for the project was derived from excavating the site itself and was supplemented with further stone materials from within a radius of 8 kilometers. Components were rammed in a nearby warehouse with a specially engineered ramming machine, which we developed at Lehm Ton Erde. This allowed the elements to be mass-produced, meeting the strict normative standards for structural capacity and material consistency in Switzerland. While in this instance our team completed these components, the machine could easily have been operated by a single technical expert and accompanied by untrained local laborers. The components carried their own load and required few expensive, imported materials to supplement the structural stability.

A fundamental willingness to build with earth was the result of a long tradition of discussing earthen architecture in Switzerland. Particularly in the 1980s and 1990s, there was a broad-based

Process

Prefabrication of rammed earth elements at Lehm Ton Erde GmbH's facilities in Laufen.

public discourse about earth as a building material. The organization IG Lehm, an association for earth building and earth building professionals, was founded in Zurich. In the early 1990s, the restaurant of the Masoala Hall of the Zurich Zoo was originally planned to have been constructed in rammed earth. ETH Professor Dr. Hans Hugi (whose assistant was the young Santiago Calatrava) began researching new approaches to traditional earth building techniques, including international collaborations in Ethiopia and Yemen. This research also resulted in a number of dissertations, of which the 1997 thesis by Thomas Kleespies remains one of the seminal investigations into the methods of *pisé* earth building today. However, in the Swiss context, while there was openness toward the use of earth, the discourse remained on a largely theoretical level, and no major companies were founded to produce earthen elements for construction.

Across the border in Vorarlberg, Austria, prior to this, I had begun to produce such elements in 1990. After several smaller architectural projects constructed using in situ rammed earth elements, such as a wall at the Landeskrankenhaus Feldkirch in 1992 and the Wil Cemetery in St. Gallen, Switzerland, in 1997, I founded Lehm Ton Erde with the intention of upscaling my practices. It was around this time that architects Herzog & de Meuron

Retouching joints between the elements of the Ricola Kräuterzentrum's façade.

became aware of Lehm Ton Erde through a project in Basel for a *Schaulager*, or warehouse to store art that is also accessible for public viewings. I initially consulted on the project in 1998. In the end, rather than constructing them with rammed earth, only the gravel excavated from the site was used in the walls for this building; the risk was deemed too significant. When approaching us in developing the Ricola Kräuterzentrum in earth many years later, this was Herzog & de Meuron's fourth iteration of the project. Each previous attempt had included a different material, but they had run into impossible challenges with every one. Timber construction was not permitted for hygienic reasons; steel was undesirable from an environmental-impact perspective; limestone bricks were too expensive. Building the Kräuterzentrum in earth—in consultation with Lehm Ton Erde—officially commenced in 2012.

One of the main challenges in the Kräuterzentrum's development was gaining the trust of the architects and the client; discussions of risk pervaded the project. A recurring theme in our own work is how previous projects engender further innovative projects and how important it is for clients and architects to gain trust in earth as a building material. In the case of the Kräuterzentrum, the project's design and legal teams went to visit another building site we were working on for the Merian Stiftung in Basel, where prefabricated rammed earth elements were being lifted into place on site. After witnessing this process, as well as successfully testing the compressive strength and stability of many material samples in the lab, they became convinced of earth's potential for the Kräuterzentrum. Lehm Ton Erde's contribution to architect Peter Stiner's Etosha House at the Basel Zoological Gardens was also a significant factor in establishing this trust. As this building had been standing for more than twelve years, it was a testament to the durability and utility of earth to withstand the Swiss climate.

Another significant challenge with the Kräuterzentrum was that there had never been such a large-scale project developed in prefabricated rammed earth components anywhere in the world. Prefabrication was necessary, in part due to the high labor costs in Switzerland, but it also addressed logistical aspects of the project. Typical for Switzerland, there was a very specific timeline for the building site. Developing the components—and then producing them en mass—required a significant amount of time, and there was little room for error. Conceiving the ramming machine for prefabrication took six months, and ramming the 670 components for the walls required eight months. This meant that part of the production had to begin before a building permit had even been issued. As such, the risk was shared by all the stakeholders in the construction process, and they were intricately involved in developing how the project would be implemented. We worked very closely with all of the project's subcontractors, from the civil engineers to the window technicians and the building physics experts involved in analyzing hygroscopic properties. The fact that this process functioned so smoothly and professionally was extremely important to the success of the project. If only the rammed earth walls had been the primary structural system, it truly would have been a best-practice example of sustainable construction and the optimization of the earth building process for the Swiss context.

Pan-Africa Housing Competition

Year: 1984
Location: Tanzania
Architect: Martin Rauch
Client: Pan-African Development Corporation
Details: unbuilt competition entry

p. 66 Proposal for building with rammed earth utilizing human labor and transportable technology for the Pan-African Housing Competition in 1984.

p. 67 This low-cost housing in rammed earth relies on common thick walls and works on a neighborhood scale.

M.R. The idea that each unique context has an appropriate balance between labor and technology originated with a competition for the Pan-African Development Corporation in 1984, just after I had finished my studies in ceramics. Primarily, the competition attempted to address the question: How can we build cheaply with unstabilized earth? It proposed a decentralized means of taking earth, which is a traditional building material on many parts of the continent, and allowing people to mechanically mix the earth and compress earthen elements by themselves. This was possible because the project proposed transporting the fabrication machine rather than the material itself. The machine would ensure a baseline quality of the unstabilized rammed earth and allow the material for an entire house to be prepared within a couple of hours. People could then invest their resources in creating quality building components and in ensuring that finished surfaces protected these elements, rather than investing their time in the physical labor of material mixing. Finally, based on shared walls and a dense built footprint, the houses could be part of an interdependent network and would require very few resources and energy sources to maintain.

Process

FUTURE ORGANIZATION OF BUILDING IN AFRICA (THE AFRICAN WAY ?)

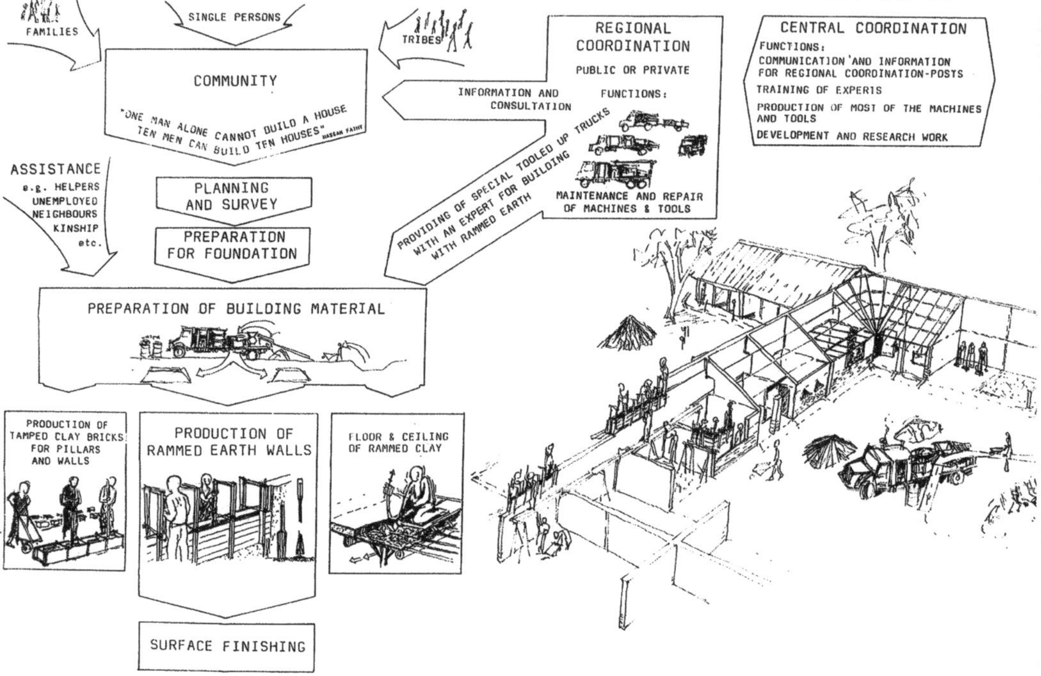

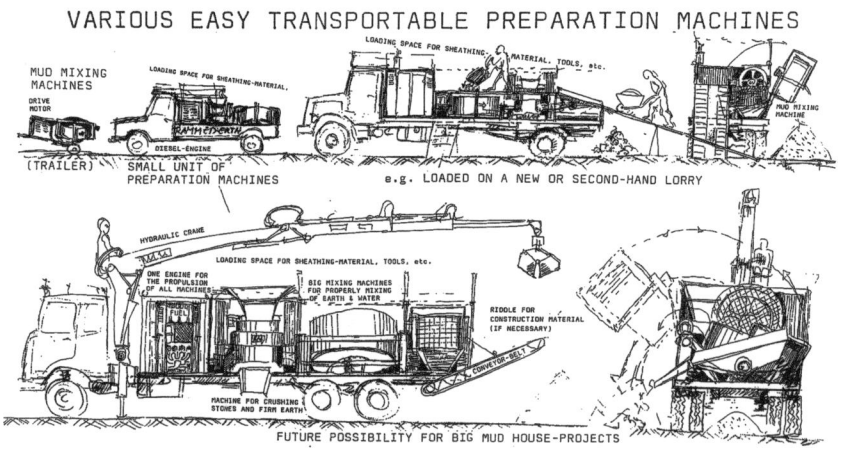

VARIOUS EASY TRANSPORTABLE PREPARATION MACHINES

Pan-Africa Housing Competition

BIRD EYE'S VIEW OF THE URBAN COMMUNITY

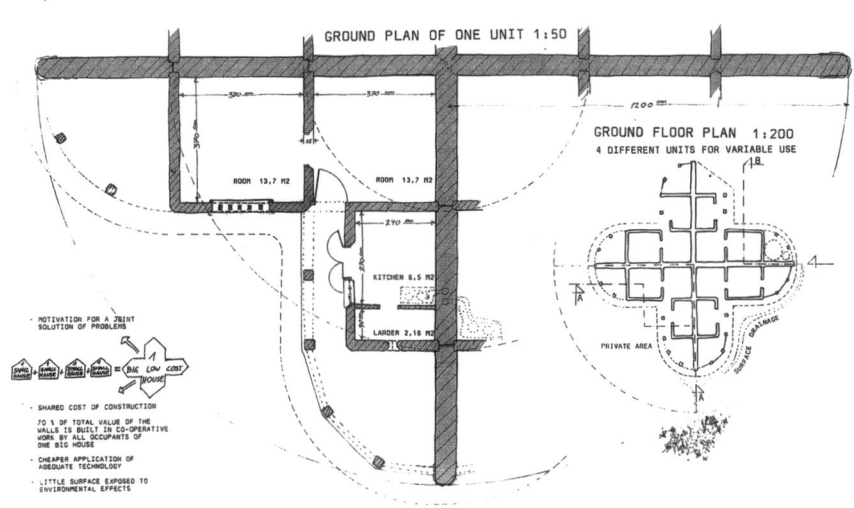

- MOTIVATION FOR A JOINT SOLUTION OF PROBLEMS
- SHARED COST OF CONSTRUCTION
- 70 % OF TOTAL VALUE OF THE WALLS IS BUILT IN CO-OPERATIVE WORK BY ALL OCCUPANTS OF ONE BIG HOUSE
- CHEAPER APPLICATION OF ADEQUATE TECHNOLOGY
- LITTLE SURFACE EXPOSED TO ENVIRONMENTAL EFFECTS

The project proposed that the machine would be organized and financed on a regional level. After the material had been produced, within a couple of days the machine could be transported to another community. Especially in places where the street network is not well constructed, the decentralized approach of providing machines to communities is much more efficient and effective than providing them with materials. The proposal approached earthen architecture as part of a social process, not just as material. The concept won first prize in the competition. However, the mid-1980s jury thought it would be impossible to implement due to corruption. Today, with the digital revolution, this idea bears reconsideration. Organizing the deployment of machines to even the most remote locations in Africa could be possible.

Another idea that originates from this time is how unnecessary it is to put any additives into the mixture when ramming earth. In our most recent project in Tanzania with the ETH Zurich, which began in 2015, local craftsmen told us how much they liked working with raw earth. They cited the quality of the construction and the solidity and stability of it after several years have passed. And, if they want to change their buildings, or completely deconstruct them, they can use the exact same material to build them anew. This would not be possible with additives. Moreover, the Tanzanian highlands are incredibly rainy. If we do not need to stabilize earth here, we do not need to do it anywhere.

Kapelle der Versöhnung

Years: 1990–2000
Location: Berlin, Germany
Architects: Rudolf Reitermann and Peter Sassenroth
Client: Evangelische Versöhnungsgemeinde Bernauerstraße
Details: in situ rammed earth, load-bearing, 180 m², 160 tons

M.R. The Berlin Kapelle der Versöhnung, or Chapel of Reconciliation, was the first in situ, load-bearing rammed earth building in Germany that had been constructed in more than ninety years. The chapel, designed by Rudolf Reitermann and Peter Sassenroth, is located in part of the no-man's-land between former East and West Berlin. It was built in place of a neo-Gothic church that had been deliberately demolished by the East German authorities in 1985 to annihilate what was perceived as a symbol of hope and freedom during the years of a divided Berlin. Earth was a highly symbolic material for this project, not just a building material: the on-site remains of the original dynamited church were folded into the new rammed earth mixture. Through the new earthen construction, it became a place for remembrance, where members of communities from around the world could

Chapel of Reconciliation in Berlin, Germany. A timber screen demarcates what was once the choir room of the site's original church.

Rammed earth encloses the inner sanctum of the space and its altar.

come together to imagine a new future. And the experience of the project had a lasting impact on those who participated—three of them actually went on to found their own earth building companies.

The original design for the church was supposed to be in concrete and steel. But the church's pastor, Pfarrer Manfred Fischer, was vehemently against the use of concrete for what was supposed to be a symbol of reconciliation in this former buffer zone. Concrete would send the wrong signal, he argued: it was a material of war. He proposed that the architects consider using earth and timber instead. This conflict between the client and the architects led the regional church in Berlin (the Berliner Landeskirche) to intervene, and they commissioned Klaus Dirks, professor at the TU Berlin and an expert in concrete construction, to convince Pfarrer Fischer and his community of the merits of concrete. Coincidentally, Klaus Dirks and I had worked together one year before on a project in Düsseldorf—a 22-meter-high, 80-meter-long, and 0.6-meter-thick rammed earth wall for the CUBUS Hotel and Offices project by schneider+schumacher. He had conducted the compressive-strength testing of our material samples for the project. This had persuaded him that earth was a viable alternative to concrete in the right context. So instead of convincing the church to use concrete, Dirks actually convinced the architects to use rammed earth. While they had initially opposed earth because they did not consider it to be a modern enough material, they were positively surprised by the projects I had realized at the time. As is so often the case with our work, it took the beauty and resilience of past projects to facilitate new advances with the material.

Once everyone was united in the decision to utilize rammed earth and timber, Klaus Dirks ensured that a building permit was secured and we began work on site in July 1999. What was particularly poignant to me at the time was the fact that the architectonic concept, which everyone involved was very enthusiastic about, remained fully intact: it was just executed with earth instead of concrete. The only major discussion that took place due to this switch was whether the 7-meter-high rammed earth walls would be permitted to act as load-bearing. The walls were proposed to be 60 centimeters thick, and the team calculating the statics suggested integrating secondary columns into the walls to meet the requirements they had been given by the permit office. But just after we began building, the load-bearing walls were certified, and, as is visible today, no further ring of timber columns around the exterior was required to support the eaves of the roof.

METI School

Years: 2004–2006
Location: Rudrapur, Bangladesh
Architects: Anna Heringer and Eike Roswag
Client: Dipshikha Society for Village Development
Details: cob earth walls reinforced with straw, load-bearing, 325 m²

A.H. I had always had a passion for earthen architecture: I was sure I would someday build earth houses even before I started studying. However, earth was not covered in our general curriculum, and I had started to think this vision was a sort of utopian dream. The moment I worked on my first earthen wall in a workshop with Martin Rauch was the moment I discovered the missing link between my passions for architecture and development work, and I immediately knew that this was *my* material. I trusted that gut instinct and decided to plan an urgently required school for the rural development NGO Dipshikha, with whom I had volunteered in Bangladesh when I was nineteen years old.

Student volunteers also participated in the process of creating the METI School they would later occupy.

Construction team at the METI School in Rudrapur, Bangladesh.

The project contained the school for children, a library, teacher accommodations, and workshops for tailors from the village of Rudrapur.

The project was made possible due to the generous funding of Shanti Partnerschaft Bangladesh e.V., and through numerous collaborations. Eike Roswag, an architect from Berlin, brought his experience and passion for technical planning to the realization process and managed the site. Emmanuel Heringer, a trained carpenter and basket weaver, invented our bamboo connections and lashing techniques. The engineering team of Christof Ziegert and Uwe Sailer conducted structural calculations. And Stefanie Haider-Heringer, a master blacksmith, supported the training of our craftsmen from Rudrapur.

When we first met the workers from the village, I was slightly intimidated. The core team of twenty mud and bamboo workers all spoke a strong dialect (and no English!); none could read a meter rule, none had ever used a level, none had ever seen an architectural drawing before. And I imagine none of them had ever had a young, female boss before—but we were able to build a great

METI School

The earth building technique used for the METI School allowed the creation of playful, cave-like spaces for the children.

deal of mutual respect through working together on the site. In the beginning, their enthusiasm was not particularly high, and I am not sure if they took our foreign team seriously. But they were happy to have a job. And the more they got involved, the more we worked side by side, and the more they began to take ownership of the project.

It always was an explicit wish of mine to have the future users—the school children—involved on the site. To this end, I had asked a team of Montessori-trained teachers, Christine Karl and Clemens Bernhard, to come to Bangladesh and supervise the children's involvement on-site in the afternoons. Not every afternoon, but quite often, there was easy work they could be

Process

The Institute of Architects in Bangladesh and the Housing and Building Research Institute of Bangladesh invited BASEhabitat from the University of Linz to conduct a hands-on workshop on contemporary earth building in Dhaka.

Certificates were issued to the project participants in Rudrapur, declaring them mud and bamboo craftsmen.

involved in, like cutting rice straw in half, making straw ropes, cladding the lintels with mud, sieving sand for the mud plaster. And they liked it! I found it highly moving to see how the children radiated pride and self-confidence. That, to me, is the best part of building—one does not just build a structure, but one builds a cohesive team and creates trust in local resources.

The diversity of the team was also incredibly rich. Along with the schoolchildren creating joyful chaos some afternoons, we also had workers with physical and mental disabilities on-site. In addition, several workers were over sixty-five years old, which never would have been permissible according to stringent European building standards. However, the site workers were very clear: "Either you take all of us or none. We belong together and we take care of each other." Surprisingly, we always found appropriate work for everyone during the construction process. This is the great advantage of building with mud: it is a very inclusive way of working, and if you have a small team of trained craftsmen and experts it is completely feasible to include a majority of untrained laborers. At the conclusion of the project, we issued certificates declaring the workers mud and bamboo craftsmen, which remain much-treasured today and are proudly presented to any visitors to the village.

A worker who builds with fired bricks is a bricklayer, one who works with wood is a carpenter, but those who work with mud, clay, and earth have no professional designation. With the METI

The space between the bamboo screen and earthen walls benefits the building's climate and provides a flexible area for the METI School's children to gather.

School project, we were able to raise awareness about mud, explaining that it requires craftsmanship just like other building materials. The care put into it, and the intent behind it, is what makes it a high-quality material. This was also reflected in the language the villagers used to describe the METI School. Normally, mud houses are called "bari," whereas they use the English word "building" for brick houses. METI is referred to as a "building."

The school had an impact as a building, and also became a catalyst for further development. It won the Aga Khan Award for Architecture in 2007, which brought a lot of attention to the building and the vision it represents. Since then, tourists from Bangladesh as well as abroad have begun to visit the school; the number of visitors is constantly increasing. And more projects ensued! For example, Martin Rauch and I conducted a workshop in Dhaka with the Institute of Architects in Bangladesh and another with BASEhabitat Linz. They aimed to train architects and engineers in modern techniques for building with earth. Since then, several of our colleagues have successfully built with mud, such as the Aga Khan Award-winning architect Marina Tabassum and renowned Bangladeshi architect Nahas Khalil. The workers from Rudrapur have also been hired for projects in other parts of Bangladesh.

In Rudrapur itself, a follow-up project called the Dipshikha Electrical Skill Improvement (DESI) building was constructed, which was a vocational training center that also won two international awards (the Swiss Solar Award and the Architectural Review's Emerging Architecture Award in 2008). In addition, three housing prototypes were built for farming families. Construction on a sixth building in the area, a center for people with disabilities and a tailor workshop designed by Studio Anna Heringer, began in 2018. In contrast to previous constructions in Rudrapur, no team of foreign experts will continuously monitor the site. Instead, a local contractor involved in the previous projects is supervising the site.

Haus Rauch

Years: 2005–2008
Location: Schlins, Austria
Architects: Boltshauser Architekten and Martin Rauch
Client: Lehm Ton Erde Baukunst GmbH
Details: in situ rammed earth walls, load-bearing, rammed earth floors, earth tiling, and plaster finishes

M.R. My house captures what to me is the essence of building. It was an attempt to reinterpret the archetype of the simple hut that I had encountered so many years before in East Africa, but for the architecture of contemporary Europe. The idea that earth excavated from a site could transform into such a luxurious architectonic object was something I wanted to prove with constructing my own home. In ancient times, both palaces and stables were built with earth; there were houses for rich and poor with the same material. I wanted to test this as a design principle, as well as to show how sustainable and resilient earth can be.

Layers of protruding tiles protect the rammed earth walls of Haus Rauch while lending it a modern aesthetic.

In building Haus Rauch, I wanted to make something that would stand the test of time and prove earth's ability to resist weathering, even in the climate of Vorarlberg. In our projects, we use *calculated erosion*, meaning that we anticipate the façade weathering by about two centimeters before the natural stones in the mixture protrude enough to preclude further runoff, and we include this in our design calculations. As a homeowner, this has a psychological impact. With other materials, one is not witness to the façade weathering in such a direct way. One can only recognize the impact much later, and not much can be done about it other than to restore or replace the material. But with earth, the weathering of the façade is visible right away. For the first two or three years, the façade changes through this weathering. Even with the knowledge of how this process works, I have to admit I was a bit nervous after three hours of driving rain, as sometimes occurs in Vorarlberg. But the most wonderful thing happens after the storm has passed and one begins to trust the material more and more. My house is as stable as solid rock. This is precisely why I feel so comfortable there. Massive constructions in earth naturally exude comfort and stability, as well as having an unsurpassed interior climate.

So much was possible in this project because I was the landowner, the client, the master builder, and the co-designer with Roger Boltshauser all in one. In other projects, there are often major questions about liability and a high level of risk that precludes innovation. But in my house I could assume responsibility for everything, so it was comparatively easy to develop and avoid the issues that had stopped innovation in projects of the past. It was an experiment, really, a chance to find out what was possible — to prove my thesis on building with untreated, unstabilized earth in Central Europe. And this was what I took away from the project more than anything else: we do not need to stabilize rammed earth.

Compared to typical building sites in Europe, specifically in the European Union, we progressed slowly — it took us over a year to construct Haus Rauch. I was once talking to a brickmaker and asked him how long it would typically take him to construct

Haus Rauch

There are no chemical additives in the earth used for Haus Rauch, meaning it can be 100 percent recycled—into new projects or back into the ground from whence it came.

Haus Rauch's interior is finished with a white earthen plaster, allowing the walls to breathe.

a house of my volume with bricks. He said it would only take half a day. Producing the earth mixture on our site took over six months. In such conversations, it becomes particularly clear that working with earth in situ is a completely different process! And it achieves a completely different result. When you remove the formwork from a rammed earth wall, the human energy put into it manifests itself before your eyes. The layers are like the striation of the earth itself. And the full impact of this power is only truly visible at the very end of the process, when the building is completed. Bricks and concrete simply do not have this symbiosis.

Plazza Pintgia Stable

Year: 2010
Location: Almens, Switzerland
Architects: gujan + pally architekten ag
Client: Marlene Gujan and Conrad Pally
Details: prefabricated, load-bearing rammed earth, 59 m², 70 tons

M.R. Earth building also has significant capacity to play a role in the renovation of historic structures; for example, Central European structures executed in wood. Wood alone typically has too little thermal mass for the European climate. Earth, as a massive material, can readily compensate this deficit. Earth is slightly less moist than wood; it simultaneously absorbs additional water vapor from the wood while preserving it, and it is even fireproof. It is also possible to work with straw-and-earth mixtures, as is traditional in the construction of half-timbered houses in Central Europe. The organic fibers of the straw in mixtures made hundreds of years ago are still just as viable as they were when the house was built. Working in this way is climatically appropriate as well as architecturally appealing.

After Haus Rauch was widely published in 2008, the architect-owners of the Plazza Pintgia Stable in the Swiss canton of Graubünden, gujan + pally, became interested in converting it to a residence with load-bearing timber and rammed earth. Together, we planned the load of the exterior façade to be carried by timber framing, and load-bearing rammed earth structures for the interior spaces. There is no steel reinforcement of any kind in the project—not even nails or screws. This therefore represents another step forward in innovation with rammed earth. And once again, progress was streamlined by the fact that the clients were also the architects and land owners. They wanted to implement rammed earth walls because of the connection between architectural form and material.

The project is also particularly innovative because it is the first residential project by Lehm Ton Erde that was prefabricated and transported to the building site. We used earth from Schlins and made the parts in our atelier. The structure of the village

The Plazza Pintgia Stable in the center of Almens, Switzerland, required prefabricated elements.

A rammed earth hearth and walls ideally complemented the wooden construction for the renovation of the stable.

core, composed of a dense web of wooden stalls from the bygone farming era, made it completely impossible to work in situ. It was even challenging for construction vehicles to access the site. We transported the prefabricated components to a large parking lot at the edge of the village, and then a special, narrower truck moved them to the building site. A custom crane was also required. The earthen walls comprised 160 elements, all of which were the same. The earth can be thermally activated over the three stories of the building through the heating-pipe system integrated into the parts. They were set at the same time that the timberwork was conducted to ensure the harmony of the overall system. The building as a whole can regulate its own interior climate, its humidity; it does not require ducts or pipes for ventilation. This made the project not only beautiful but also financially feasible. This speaks to its inherent quality as an ecological material.

Schweizerische Vogelwarte

Years: 2013–2014
Location: Sempach, Switzerland
Architects: :mldz Architekten
Client: Swiss Ornithological Institute
Details: prefabricated, non-load-bearing rammed earth walls, 1,240 m², 1,130 tons

Corten steel window frames were installed with the rammed earth façade in Sempach.

M.R. The symbolic as well as the aesthetic qualities of earth were behind selecting it for the façade of the Swiss Ornithological Institute in Sempach, Switzerland. This institute is run by an organization of more than one hundred bird enthusiasts and was founded during the early years of the environmental movement in the 1960s and 1970s. Protecting birds from pesticides like DDT was actually one of the earliest campaigns of this movement, so the environmental impact of the building was a very significant factor in its design, as well as its appearance, which had to be as natural as possible for the well-being of the bird population. The building for the visitor's center was advertised as a competition, and we began collaborating with :mldz, the center's architects, during this early planning phase.

For Lehm Ton Erde, this project presented a new opportunity to test how earthen façades react to intense weathering conditions. The institute is located directly on a lake, and the rain always storms across the water directly onto the primary façade. Every year since the project was constructed, we have had a meeting with all parties involved—including a couple of lawyers—to measure how much the wall has eroded. While in Haus Rauch the speed breakers in the façade were tiles that protruded by sever-

Schweizerische Vogelwarte

The visitor center of the Swiss Ornithological Station lies on Sempach Lake, comprising two compact structures joined by a foyer.

al centimeters, in projects like this and Ricola we implemented the breakers with trass lime to achieve a more fluid visual concept and push the boundaries of what is possible with earth. This system is initially flush with the plane of the façade, so there has to be some erosion before it becomes truly effective. So far, all erosion has remained within the figures we precalculated, but the façade is eroding faster than would be typical with protruding elements because of the driving rain and wind coming off the lake. Even when the erosion has been calculated and is inherent to the long-term strength of the walls, it is understandably difficult for a client to simply await this process, watching their building erode.

Process

Training Centre for Sustainability

Year: 2010
Location: Chwitter / Marrakesh, Morocco
Architects: Martin Rauch and Anna Heringer, with Nägele Waibel architects and Salima Naji
Client: Fondation Allience, Alami
Details: unbuilt competition entry

Perforated tile elements, created in collaboration with Karak Tiles, were designed to characterize the façade of the Training Centre outside Marrakesh.

A.H. Our work often encounters the legacy of juxtapositions between local traditions and imported standards; for example, in Morocco. It is one of the countries with the most well-established and well-preserved earth building cultures, yet there are continual efforts to avoid earth in contemporary constructions. Rather than further developing earth as a material, thereby elevating it to modern standards, buildings are often executed in concrete and finished to resemble earthen architecture. This mentality even permeates building codes, for example in Marrakesh, where new buildings must be colored externally in earth tones and are not allowed to be built taller than a palm tree.

In 2014, Martin Rauch and I partnered with Nägele Waibel architects and Salima Naji to win a competition for a new school of sustainable construction in Chwitter, a satellite town outside Marrakesh. The project aimed to show the potential formal and technical development of kasbahs, the rural fortresses constructed with rammed earth across Morocco. We carefully analyzed the spatial sequences of traditional Moroccan structures, their proportions, their dramaturgy. The spaces of a kasbah, the atmospheric quality of its interior courtyards and niches, and the playful use of ornaments and water elements in traditional Moroccan architecture inspired our design. But it was connected with a modern lifestyle, reflecting the aspirations and requirements of contemporary times.

The project was also an attempt at authenticity, in formulating a sense of identity connected to the place's history through local materials and climatic specificities. Why should earthen or wooden details be cast of concrete and painted over, or glass and steel façades be utilized in a desert climate? Merely be-

Training Centre for Sustainability

Ancient earth building techniques in Morocco, as seen in a fortress-like kasbah.

Modern buildings in Morocco are typically concrete, yet painted to resemble earthen architecture.

This competition entry interprets the traditional Moroccan *ksar* and contemporary *madrasa* to create a Training Centre for Sustainable Design.

Tiles protuding from the façade of the Training Centre intended to create a linear architectural expression.

cause they are perceived as more modern? Or because there are powerful capital-driven forces behind industrialized materials? Modernity should not be about the "newness" of a material or a process, but rather our creative ability to use our resources in novel ways. As such, we proposed executing the construction with local rammed earth. The exterior walls included what we call horizontal "speed breakers" to slow the flow of rainwater, impeding the erosion of the façade.

Climate simulations showed that the massive walls would retain a great deal of heat, and we required a shading system. We met this challenge by designing the speed breakers with ceramic tiles that protruded 25 centimeters out of the façade. This was not only a way to innovate with rammed earth but also to interpret traditional ornamentation for a contemporary architectonic expression. The tiles were created with an ornate perforation, which not only helped them to cool more rapidly but also created a flowing ornament of shadows on the face of the building, continually changing its appearance with the passage of time. Unfortunately, the project has not yet been built.

King Abdulaziz Centre for World Culture

Years: 2010–2014
Location: Dhahran, Saudi Arabia
Architects: Snøhetta
Client: Aramco
Details: prefabricated rammed earth walls, non-load-bearing, 2,823 m², 3,009 tons

M.R. The King Abdulaziz Centre for World Culture in Saudi Arabia is the largest earth building ever constructed in modern times, and the first time rammed earth has been deployed as an architectonic element at this scale. This project also evolved through the competition process: the Norwegian architectural office Snøhetta developed their contribution in consultation with us at Lehm Ton Erde. It represents an interesting compromise in rammed earth construction, in which an extremely complex building requires a high degree of technology, yet these demands exist in a cultural context where labor is inexpensive. In Saudi Arabia, it was therefore more efficient to use large teams in the production process than to ram with machines.

Saudi Arabia has a storied tradition of building with earth; one of the royal palaces in Riyadh was built of earth to mimic the shape of a tent, for example. However, earth buildings were often not well maintained. In the 1970s, many structures were demolished and replaced with concrete constructions. By implementing new projects, trust in the material could be reestablished, and there is now a very high interest in working with earth once more. Lehm Ton Erde was responsible for the load-bearing exterior walls and also acted as a general contractor on the site. The clients and architectural team were convinced to use earth when they visited the Ricola Kräuterzentrum building site. There, we conducted a three-day workshop with them to prove the compressive strength and demonstrate how it could be logistically coordinated on a large-scale, complex building site. We were really considered exotic by the local teams in Saudi Arabia, because they just could not imagine how the ramming process was supposed to work. Ten or fifteen engineers looked at the formwork and could not believe that we were building with unstabilized earth, without any kind of chemical additives or integrated

One-to-one scale mock-ups were built for the King Abdulaziz Centre for World Culture to test the quality of the earth and conceive the aesthetic concept.

Process

More than 150 people worked on the building site of the King Abdulaziz Centre for eight months.

The retouching process at the King Abdulaziz Centre allowed for seamless joints between rammed earth elements, as well as between these prefabricated components and other building parts such as steel framing.

reinforcement. Only after we made 1:1 scale mock-ups — one in earth and one in earth with a cement additive — were they finally convincedd that reinforcement was unnecessary. And once they had seen how we worked on the Kräuterzentrum, they were also convinced that rammed earth was exactly the right material for their project.

The building site was actually akin to European standards in regard to the dimensions of the project and the quality required for the material. We planned it from Austria, but we built it with people in Saudi Arabia. We utilized the same process, but people did the ramming instead of a machine. Six employees of Lehm Ton Erde went to the site for eight months to manage the construction process, in which the components were prefabricated and crane-lifted into place. One person managed the prefabrication, two managed the lifting, and three managed the retouching and finishing of the wall. And there were 150 people working with them! In total, over 7,000 people were on the building

site—it was like working in a thriving ant's nest compared to our previous building sites, where the ratio of technical experts to workers was more like 1:10. Here, in Saudi Arabia, it was usually more like 1:30 or 1:50. But it is important to note that this is actually because labor is too cheap. The people there were exploited. It was not just for the earth elements of the building design that everything was done by hand. While it was an incredibly positive experience to see how such a massive project could be realized primarily through human labor, we were setting twelve to thirteen elements during the night, when it was cooler, with twenty to thirty people at a time. These are very extreme working conditions.

The process would never be possible in this way in Europe, where labor is more expensive and there are far fewer people that have craftsman experience. In Saudi Arabia, we had a lot of workers of Pakistani and Filipino origin who had previously worked with earth and had an affinity for the material and the process. They had immense skill in retouching the wall after the prefabricated elements were set, and this craftsmanship is tangible in the final built product.

People were also surprised how well the connection between earth and other building materials worked. Earth can easily be joined with steel, chrome, and glass—prefabricated parts can be retouched with the same care that we would use to seal the joints between rammed earth components in an unstabilized wall. Through the retouching process, the steel edges of the glazed areas in the walls could be finished so precisely with earth in a way that never would have been possible with other prefabricated materials and modular systems. And this can be done with any kind of form, whether linear or more organic!

Alnatura Arbeitswelt

Years: 2016–2017
Location: Darmstadt, Germany
Architects: haas cook zemmrich STUDIO250
Client: Campus 360 GmbH / Alnatura
Details: prefabricated rammed earth walls with integrated insulation, non-load-bearing, 13,500 m²

M.R. Along with the Ricola Kräuterzentrum, the Alnatura Arbeitswelt project is one of our most technical to date. Alnatura wanted to create a new campus for their headquarters, with over 13,500 square meters of floor space for 500 employees. We were able to procure 60 percent of our earth from the excavations for Stuttgart 21—a contested building project to accommodate high-speed trains underground—which would have otherwise been considered an unusable byproduct of the building site. To create the prefabricated parts on the building site, six people ran a machine to ram the earth with an integrated layer of insulation. The three-story, 12-meter-high walls were not the load-bearing structural system for the entire project, but they carried their own load. And because of the integrated insulation, sandwiched between two layers of earth, the raw material was visible from the inside as well as the outside. This is a significant innovation

Alnatura Arbeitswelt

Setting the prefabricated rammed earth elements of the Alnatura Arbeitswelt project.

Exterior of the Alnatura Arbeitswelt office building, the heart of Alnatura's "campus," has 13,500 square meters of office space.

in regard to upscaling earth as a prefabricated product, as well as an advance in formulating an architectural language for the material.

As we at Lehm Ton Erde began to discuss the appearance of the façade with the client and the architects, haas cook zemmrich STUDIO2050, we decided mutually that the earth should be visible everywhere. Then, its properties would be just as beneficial inside to the back-office employees as they would be on the exterior. However, we also had to achieve a U-value—which describes the rate of heat transferred through a building component—of at least 30 in accordance with German regulations, and this was only possible with additional insulation. Once again, in our typical fashion of applied research, we tested innovation through a specific project. We first developed three rammed-earth elements as an experiment, and then all of the technical experts on the project came together to plan how it should evolve. There was a certain level of risk for each subcontractor, as well as for Lehm Ton Erde. For example, we agreed to assume some of the financial risk in developing the specialized ramming machine with the clients. We designed the machine six months before production was scheduled to begin, and the client agreed to cover 70 percent of these costs. We contributed the other 30 percent of the finances and collaborated directly with the mechanical engineering firm to develop our ideas about what the ramming machine should do and how it should work.

However, it was not the technical innovation that ended up as our greatest challenge on the Alnatura project—it was getting the required certification for the machine. This was an extremely drawn-out process, which also required significant financial investment by Lehm Ton Erde and involved an incredible amount of administrative work. Regulations often pose a gigantic hurdle for innovation in earth building. If we were developing a machine that we were planning to manufacture thousands of times for sale, the costs and administration would be appropriate. But for a single machine developed for a single project, these regulatory aspects nearly halted conceptual development entirely.

OMICRON Monolith

Year: 2014
Location: Klaus, Austria
Architects: Anna Heringer and Martin Rauch
Client: OMICRON AG
Details: zabour earth walls reinforced with geotextile webbing and clay vessels, load-bearing, 80 m², 33 tons

A.H. The project Martin Rauch and I executed for OMICRON is an example of a high-manpower and low-tech approach in a European context. OMICRON is an international electrical engineering company that provides testing, diagnosis, and monitoring solutions for electrical energy systems. The OMICRON Development Center is located in a small village in Vorarlberg, near the Swiss-Austrian border. As a result of the continuous growth of the company and their team, the existing premises were expanded to provide space for 200 additional workplaces and other facilities. The company is known for their high regard for corporate social responsibility, and they support a number of projects in developing countries. This includes two projects by Studio Anna Heringer: the DESI building in Bangladesh and a kindergarten in Zimbabwe. Their intention was to bring a little bit of this global atmosphere into their new office building, designed by Dietrich Untertrifaller, through interventions by different architects and designers.

The design for the Monolith emerged out of a process Martin and I call "claystorming"—a stream-of-consciousness method we developed over the past couple of years through our joint projects. It is an intuitive design process conducted through hand-shap-

Constructing the OMICRON Monolith by hand, layer by layer, was a meditative process in which the company's employees actively participated. The project consisted of three elements intended to act as a "living room" for employees.

Process

ing clay models. The area selected for our intervention was one of the building's atrium spaces. Martin and I were commissioned to design a relaxation space for the employees to hang out, rest, or chat over a fair-trade coffee. As a counterpoint to the visual transparency of the office spaces, our design concept provided the employees of OMICRON a place for a contemplative retreat. We designed a two-story structure, with niches upstairs for power naps and a womb-like seating area on the ground level with light falling from above.

Since we did not have to take weathering into account, it was a great opportunity to test a free-form shape, fully exploring the more formally expressive characteristics of clay. The appropriate technique for this sculptural approach was zabour, which works without any formwork. It is one of the most basic building techniques used in many parts of the world. The technique itself is my personal favorite—it is so physical. One shapes the

The entry to the enclosed, geode-like Monolith is complemented by a more public sitting space, the Groundcave, completed with polished earth plaster.

Seating in the Monolith's interior, created with the zabour earth building technique. The hand-stitched and printed cushions were custom made by the women of Rudrapur, where the METI School catalyzed this development.

The Monolith's dome was constructed using hollow ceramic vessels, which stiffened the earthen mixture.

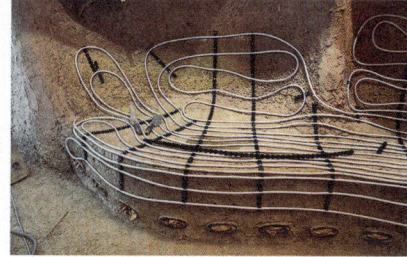

Although it may appear simplistic, the Monolith includes lighting, airflow, tubing, and acoustic features such that music can be played and the mood adjusted to suit the current occupants.

The three elements of the OMICRON "living room" included the Monolith, Groundcave, and Zeppelin.

Process

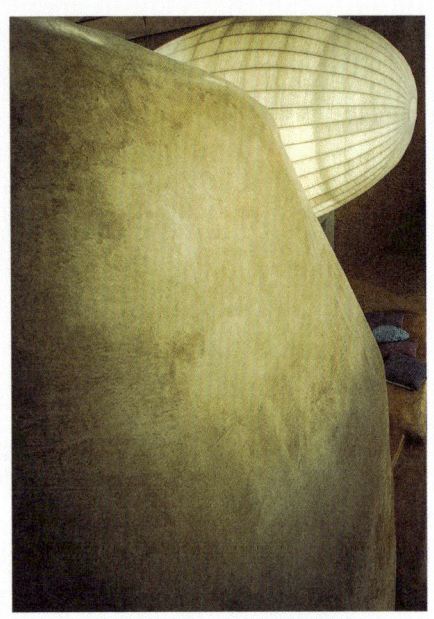

Human labor was used to create the Monolith's polished finish.

The Zeppelin is a meeting space that is illuminated when it is dark outside, contrasting to the solidity of the Monolith.

form physically, by hand. It connects to something archaic, to build a structure by hand; it is empowering. The wet mud, mixed with a small amount of stones and natural fibers, is shaped in layers, akin to shaping a ceramic vessel. The only difference is that our vessel was two stories high! And we also had a special challenge: the structure was built on the second floor, on top of a ceiling that could not bear much of a load.

So we improvised—artistically as well as structurally. The first step was to reduce the thickness of the walls of our form to 15 centimeters and to stiffen them with vertical ribs, like a bell pepper. We also used geotextile webbing for horizontal reinforcement and included a metal ring, added to increase tensile strength and bear the load of the inner dome. The dome itself was also a special challenge: to keep it as light as possible, we fortified the vaulted form with hollow ceramic pots, fired in a kiln for extra strength and stability. The combination of the clay's elasticity and the hardened ceramics allowed us to freely shape the structure as we went. And this also affected the aesthetics of the final product: the fired pots are visible from below, act as a form of acoustic absorption, and contain lighting elements. We were able to achieve maximum comfort throughout the atrium by also integrating water tubes for cooling into the floor and walls and heating into the interior seating niches.

In this project, we showcased how earth could be used for several different functions. First, it was the load-bearing structure of the Monolith. Then, instead of using acoustic panels to dampen sound, we applied a rough finish of clay plastering with cork. For the surface of the floor, we added casein to the mixture in order to create surfaces without any joints. Casein is a natural substance derived from milk protein and results in a seamless, waxy surface. The finished product is not only visually appealing but also creates a perfect moisture-vapor balance. While the rough interior surface enhanced the Monolith's archaic character, we wanted the outside to shine, like a precious stone. But rather than applying wax as a finish, as would have been easiest, we wanted to allow the surface of the Monolith to breathe. Ceramics teach us that polishing wet clay at the right moment, with the right pressure and speed, results in a shiny surface. And this is what we did. We invited company employees, friends, and family to rub the mud until it shone! I loved how out of simple dirt, with time and patience and manual skills, such a precious architectonic object could be formed.

Reflecting on this project actually provokes me in retrospect, because from an economic and common-sense perspective building this way should be inexpensive. The material is so widely available and so low-cost, it only requires human labor to shape, and this results in job creation. But in countries like Austria, it would have actually been cheaper to 3D-print our design with a cement-based material or plastic polymers. Something is fundamentally amiss with our socioeconomic system if this is the case. A system that does not consider the negative impact of a material, and therefore the true cost of construction—one which taxes human labor but not carbon emissions or machines—is simply not sustainable.

Mud WORKS! The 2016 Venice Biennale

Year: 2016
Location: Venice, Italy
Authors: Anna Heringer, Martin Rauch, and Andres Lepik
Client: Alejandro Aravena / La Biennale de Venezia
Details: zabour earth walls reinforced with geotextiles, load-bearing

A.H. Building with earth has become a part of architectural discourse over the past several years. This was one of the reasons we were invited by Alejandro Aravena to participate in the 2016 Venice Biennale, in collaboration with Andres Lepik from the Technical University of Munich. In an e-mail to me, he asked: "What is a battle you would like to present at the Biennale?" The thing that immediately came to mind was how, in each and every one of our projects, we constantly have to contend with fears about our material. Whether you call it earth, mud, or clay, it is seen as vulnerable and ephemeral.

We conceived our contribution to the Biennale as a form of acupuncture, in which visitors from all over the world could gain a direct, physical experience of the material: they could see and feel its strength and stability, its range of aesthetic characters—polished, rough, its nuanced colors—and its different techniques. Our installation contained a rammed earth floor, an in situ rammed earth bench, a prefabricated rammed earth panel,

Anna Heringer, Martin Rauch, and Andres Lepik's contribution to the 2016 Venice Architecture Biennale, entitled Mud WORKS!, included a monolith nicknamed Pepita, a polished rammed earth floor, rammed earth panels, and information about earth building.

Mud WORKS! The 2016 Venice Biennale

Pepita consists solely of unstabilized earth.

Recyclable geotextile webbing was used to stiffen Pepita's dome rather than chemical additives.

Pepita's demolition allowed its earth to be recycled for several further projects.

and a monolithic object derived from our OMICRON Monolith, executed with the zabour technique. We wanted to provide exhibition visitors with the possibility to inhale the deeply archaic and emotionally warm yet physically cool atmosphere on the inside of the mud sculpture that we nicknamed "Pepita."

Our predominant construction challenge was an Italian law that made acquiring a building permit for load-bearing earthen structures extremely difficult. This kind of prohibition against earth as load-bearing building material is happening quietly across more and more countries—for example, Colombia and Nicaragua—all of them countries with a long tradition of building with earth. Earth alone is not seismically safe—just as concrete alone is not safe. Earth must be reinforced, for example with timber, steel and concrete, geotextile mesh, or bamboo. There are a vast number of traditional building types that have survived centuries of earthquakes, and there are also projects in Haiti—by CRAterre, for example—which are paradigms of how to build with earth in earthquake-prone areas. In Italy, the law does not differentiate between seismic regions. Sardinia, for example, with its storied tradition of earth houses, is not in an earthquake zone, yet buildings on the island have to satisfy the law anyway. For Venice, the advice from the Biennale, at first, was to erect a timber structure cladded with clay plaster on chicken-wire mesh instead. But we certainly could not agree to build a fake mud structure! Instead, we reinforced our "Pepita" with horizontal layers of geotextiles. Similar to our project for OMICRON, the walls were thin and strengthened with structural, vertical ribs. Officially, it had to be called an "artwork," not a building.

The Biennale was a formative experience, and our contribution was widely discussed. The process of dismantling "Pepita" also provided a chance to test how stable the structure was. We weakened it by constantly widening holes in its sides. The walls were far stronger than we originally expected! This process also showed how well the connection between the geotextiles and the mud worked. As a final step, we collected all the mud in barrels for further projects. In the meantime, the material has already been recycled twice—for the 2017 Art Biennale, by

Interior of Pepita, created with the zabour earth building technique.

Mariechen Danz; and for the 2018 Venice Architecture Biennale, both by Marina Tabassum and for the Chilean pavilion.

The deconstruction process is relevant to each and every one of our projects. In fact, in the future each project could be required to include a "deconstruction plan" when applying for a building permit. For most of the projects, it would be a simple process. First, spray the walls with water and let them crumble. Then, remove all of the pipes and technical installations, the windows, and any other elements that have been part of the construction, such as a ring beam. Finally, break down the remaining earthen substance and fold it back into the ground of the building site. It would not even contaminate the groundwater.

RoSana Health Center and Guesthouse
Year: 2021
Location: Rosenheim, Germany
Authors: Anna Heringer and Martin Rauch
Client: Heidi und Sören Gutschmidt
Details: rammed earth walls with mud plastering and mud-casein floors

AH: The RoSana Guesthouse retreat is located near an old mill in Rosenheim, next to an alluvial forest and ensconced by two branches of the Mangfall River. The building was designed to accommodate one staff member and five guests, who typically stay at the center for several weeks with almost no external distractions. This means they experience the building immersively and intensely.

The guesthouse is not orthogonal but rather meanders along the edge of the forest and nestles into the wild, organic growth. From the pathway on the river, it looks more like a nest than a building—and that was precisely the intention when Martin and I designed it.

There are so many resources given to us by nature for free, if we are only sensitive enough to see them and creative enough to utilize them. The rooms are therefore composed of but a few

RoSana Health Center and Guesthouse

The RoSana Guesthouse in Rosenheim is designed to be as healthy as possible, both for people and the planet.

Rammed earth and timber details characterize the building throughout.

materials: rammed earth walls, mud plastering, mud-casein floors, handcrafted ceramics, and tadelakt on a load-bearing timber frame. Casein is a traditional organic glue made out of milk and lime—and thus fully ecological. Using it on floors is a new technique, which was developed and practiced by craftspeople trained on the project.

This simplicity and the subtle nuances of material choices showcase the diverse ways of working with earth, calming the mind while opening the senses. The casein floors and clay plastering bring warmth and colorful accents into the rooms. The guesthouse is proof that quality is not a matter of size and or square meterage, but rather, it is a matter of quality, of well thought-out spatial proportions and handcrafted, natural building materials.

What is designing but making a series of decisions? How much mass can the site accept? How high, how dense, what feels appropriate? In our experience, the best decisions are born of a gut instinct. When Martin and I design, we let go of our egos, our aspirations, and instead connect with our intuition and the genius loci of the place we are working. The ideas that come to mind flow directly into our hands, as we use clay to give our intuition three-dimensional shape. We worked on RoSana until it felt right. And the project is indeed so beautiful, innovative, and ecologically advanced it won a New European Bauhaus Award in 2021, in the category "Solutions for the co-evolution of the built environment and nature!"

Process

ERDEN Werkhalle

Year: 2022
Location: Schlins, Austria
Authors: Martin Rauch, Lehm Ton Erde Baukunst GmbH
Client: Lehm Ton Erde Baukunst GmbH
Details: prefabricated, rammed earth walls

MR: Lehm Ton Erde has been constructing a new workshop since 2019. It contains our company's offices and a large-scale production hall for the manufacture of prefabricated rammed earth walls. It is not just a flagship project because it pushes all sorts of earth building techniques forwards, but because the building itself is such an ecologically innovative structure.

The main raw building material—the earth—was sourced regionally, from building site excavations. Its heating systems rely on solar energy, and the corresponding activation of massive construction elements for passive heating and cooling. The workshop also utilizes hydroelectric power from a canal along the edge of the site. This runs the experimental machines that can mass-produce rammed earth prefabricated parts.

The rammed earth elements for the buliding were thus produced directly in the workshop, and combined with other earth building techniques and complementary materials like wood. The building's dimensions are 67 by 24 meters, supported by a hybrid timber-construction frame and 67 meter-long rammed

One of the main elements of the workshop is the automatic ramming machine named "Roberta."

The exterior façade reflects the vernacular building styles of the surrounding urban fabric.

ERDEN Werkhalle

earth wall. From the façade, with its modern interpretation of the timber-framed house, to its interior joints and load-bearing rammed earth walls, the workshop represents a significant step forward in technical progress without eschweing the original handcrafted spirit of the materials.

In this space, we have started producing ERDEN PURE Walls, which are prefabrticated and unstabilized rammed earth elements for a circular building economy. They are created up to 50 meters long and 1.4 meters high, and then segmented to meet site and transportation requirements. They can be made as thin as seven centimeters, for example for interior paneling, or as thick as necessary for load-bearing walls.

With this approach, we are attempting to make rammed earth more circular and economically competitive for the building sector. We work with the company Kessler to extract raw materials for rammed earth from site excavations. We can reclaim about 60 percent, and because there is absolutely no cement in ERDEN PURE Walls, this substance can be completely recycled again by simply adding water. The mass production of these structural elements allowed us to cut costs by 50 percent and lead times by 65 percent.

Like RoSana, the highly sustainble and innovative ERDEN PURE Walls won a New European Bauhaus Award in 2021, in the category "Techniques, materials and processes for construction and design." Now that we have a competitive product, what remains to discover is how we can continue to fine-tune and upscale the process until we are able to truly make a social and environmental impact.

A Path Forward

The process of making earthen projects is edified through cumulative knowledge, close collaboration with clients to build trust, and striking the correct balance between available resources and cutting-edge technologies to create beautiful, durable objects. The projects discussed in this chapter are exemplary attempts to edify the process of building with earth. Each represents a further step toward our collective vision of earth as a material, a process, and a catalyst.

The concepts behind the Pan-Africa Housing Competition show how high-manpower and relatively low-technology contexts can be enriched through appropriate architecture. In some places, human hands are just as valuable as machines. If no resources or machinery are available, there are still ways with which we can work for and with people. This is the philosophy espoused by Anna Heringer's series of projects in Bangladesh. They represent one end of the gradient between labor and technology as focused around development cooperation, and the catalyst nature of such projects can apply to a wide variety of contexts.

Creating high-quality rammed earth projects by hand in the European context, using the manpower of untrained laborers, was proven by one of Martin Rauch's early projects, the Chapel of Reconciliation in Berlin. It is a flagship project in several senses. From a material perspective, it advances the full potential of rammed earth as the primary load-bearing structural system in a culturally symbolic public building. It also utilized participation and human labor in the construction process. Finally, as an architectonic object, it embodies a highly modern aesthetic while radiating physical warmth, as well as being tangibly emotive, evoking the spirit of collaborative building. Haus Rauch showcases the potentials of building with rammed earth in European climates and building cultures. It is also infused with creative ways of working with earth in combination with other materials, in particular with wood. As projects such as the Plazza Pintgia Stable or Alnatura Arbeitswelt prove, material combinations result in the design of efficient, stable structural systems.

For practitioners of earth building, every project involves not just calculated erosion but calculated risk. The philosophy of Anna Heringer and Martin Rauch is to push innovation at least one step further with each of their works; to tackle another highly complex challenge, but at the same time to plan in such a way that if a particular innovative aspect fails the project can still continue without risk to the client. Because it can be retouched and repaired, it is actually possible to mitigate risk with earth.

To sum up the insight derived from the works of Heringer and Rauch: industrializing the production process of rammed earth poses one of the greatest opportunities for realizing our collective vision of a building culture across the gradient between labor and technology. While innovations in rammed earth have primarily been outlined in this chapter with projects in highly industrialized, European contexts, projects are also being implemented to different degrees of technological intensity worldwide. As built-environment professionals increasingly recognize that their material choices have a lasting impact on the natural world, aspects such as embodied energy and recycling will continue to become more important in the future. Despite its perceived vulnerability, earth is actually one of the world's most resilient building materials. Even in an upscaling of the production process, and with higher degrees of prefabrication, the most beneficial properties of earth remain intact. It is flexible, forgiving, and it can be adapted over time. To this end, we must continue to consider the wider implications of our building culture and forge a path forward to enable the continued development of earthen architecture in its manifold forms.

Catalyst

From a socio-technical perspective, earth is not just a material; it is a process and can be a catalyst for development. This is because earth is as much an attitude toward sociocultural practices and building cultures as it is the embodiment of environmentally and economically responsible construction. An upscaling of earth, which improves the quality of the substance and increases its use, will amplify its positive ramifications for both people and the planet. We believe that, while earth may not be part of a highly profitable lobby, it may be able to act as a catalyst for new markets, new alliances across sectors of the design and building industries, and new socially oriented objectives that emerge in the name of sustainable building.

This chapter first examines the potential political frameworks and economic impact of earth, in the sense that despite being one of the few truly green building materials that exists on the planet it essentially remains a discarded byproduct of standard construction methods. The discussion envisages the market that rammed earth construction could generate on a larger, potentially even global scale, via prefabricated elements. In particular, because it can be adjusted to widely different contextual demands of labor and technology and work in combination with other building materials—as illustrated through the works of Anna Heringer and Martin Rauch in the previous chapter—earth can address a wide spectrum of requirements in an appropriate manner. After imagining these potentials, we then discuss the social-impact opportunities associated with more prevalent building with earth and which actors might come together in light of its uniquely sustainable qualities.

New Political Frameworks

One of the primary impediments to upscaling earth at present is the cost of labor in industrialized contexts. But this problem is not inherent to earth building. It is a product of extractive socio-economic systems regulated by politics. Profit-driven, late-stage capitalism perpetuates consumption;

corporations relying on fossil fuels receive discounts and subsidies from governments—generating enormous financial returns even during global pandemics—while we try to "tech" our way out of the climate emergencies these products and operations generate. It is simply no longer socially nor environmentally sustainable that tax and subsidy systems should be linked to profits and company bottom lines. Instead, incentives and taxation should be reframed around the idea of human labor as a source of energy, while promoting upscaling and recyclable materials.

First and foremost, subsidies for any company or product utilizing fossil fuels should cease immediately, and be replaced with incentives for change. In a 2019 WWF report on climate protection in Germany, the authors note the economic potential of decarbonizing the concrete and cement industries, because this progressive development would position the industries as international market leaders.[1] The report identified several ways to do so on both political and economic levels, including: creating financial incentives for less fossil-fuel-intensive forms of concrete, updating construction laws and standards to include aspects of climate protection, defining progressively increasing minimum standards for cement production, considering climate protection in the awarding of public contracts, and allocating higher rankings to the footprint of building materials in the certification processes of architecture and civil engineering.[2]

This discussion alludes to the need to consider full life cycles of building materials, throughout the entire design, construction, occupation, and recycling phases. Dirk Hebel, a professor of sustainable construction at Karlsruhe Institute of Technology, discussed in an interview how the building sector in the European Union is responsible for 36 percent of total solid waste production—most of which comprises excavation and demolition. If this much waste is generated, it means architects have ascribed too little value to building materials and components; in its often-singular use of elements and lack of recyclability, the built environment represents a mass failure of design. Hebel's research into the "urban mining" of upcycling building components has led him to conclude that one of the ways we have planned badly is in the use of composite materials. He noted:

> Concrete is essentially a *composite material*, composed of gravel, sand, and cement, because we do not have the technology yet to reprocess these substances and revert them to their

original state. At present, it is a *cascading material*, meaning that, essentially, 'recycled' concrete is only kicking the can down the road. This is not the solution, because we are passing on the problem to the next generation of building materials.[3]

The aforementioned WWF report echoes these findings, concluding that it is not enough to examine greenhouse gas emissions during the service phase of buildings; the construction materials themselves must be considered. Legal requirements regarding the climate footprint of building materials, the authors posit, would provide incentives for both designers and their clients to reorient their thinking towards a circular economy.[4]

However, terms from the WWF report like "climate protection" and the corresponding suggestions for change remain vague; who is involved and how these processes are designed will determine whether change is catalyzed. As the same study points out, the Emissions Trading System (ETS) was supposed to be the key policy initiative to reduce greenhouse gas emissions in the European Union.[5] However, it has not contributed to reductions in the concrete and cement industry, because it is classified as "vulnerable to carbon leakage" and thus receives carbon credits for free. These kinds of loopholes simply cannot be allowed if a circular economy is to be created in Europe and beyond.

We assert that not only should circularity be incentivized, but that once-off building components should be heavily taxed. Why should materials that harm our common future more not be taxed at higher rates, and awarded lower values in the very ratings systems with which we quantify sustainability? A system could be implemented along a scale related to how much energy is required for their production. Materials like earth — which have longer life cycles, comprise fewer toxic substances, and can be fully recycled — should receive the most subsidies, rather than the least. Such a socio-political stance would also connect to supporting human labor, which is actually the most sustainable form of energy that can be put into constructing our built environment.

Hebel believes there is a path forward for establishing a socially and environmentally just circular economy in the building sector. He identified two requirements for doing so:

First, we have to utilize non-composite materials, which can easily be reconverted into their original states. Earth is an example of this, because it is water soluble, and can then be reused in precisely the same quality as it was before. Second, we must be able to store enough components that it is easy to manage the supply of building elements without generating waste in the process. The same principle applies again: utilizing noncompound materials, such that every element can be incorporated into this circularity.[6]

Environmentally damaging practices should be taxed at higher rates. These principles of valuing human labor, providing new incentives, and new tax regimes has implications beyond the building sector.

New Markets

Maintaining the financial viability of the construction industry presents a major opportunity for the advancement of earth building. Innovation from the private sector creates significant economic pressure and slowly shifts mindsets—consider the solar-power movement or the current push for electric vehicles, both of which originated with technological innovation. This is especially relevant when defining sustainability as using as few resources as possible, seeking to maximize every possible return from every material. In Paris, for instance, the city authorities are currently trying to fight against escalating real-estate prices by digging deeper and deeper to accommodate buildings and infrastructure. Most of the city sits on high-quality earth, with excellent properties for construction; nearly two million tons of excavated material are deposited per year outside Paris, in Villeneuve-sous-Dammartin, ten kilometers away from Charles de Gaulle Airport. Over 90 percent of this excavated material could instead be tied into a new and innovative market for sustainable building.[7]

Instead, material that would be valuable for rammed earth construction remains the byproduct of current construction processes: a discarded substance considered to have no further value. Earth naturally containing clay and stones is useless to the gravel or brick industry and is simply abandoned or deposited elsewhere. However, it is a highly valuable resource for rammed earth production. Excavated material can be extracted in accordance with locally available energy resources, fully manually or by the construction industry, and either sold or given away instead of discarded. For example, construction-site managers could begin to tie the material into their cycles of production, storing and reselling the earth they excavate from building sites. Or, they could make it widely available to those seeking to build in their local area—individuals, communities, or organizations. Both of these approaches would imbue the raw material with increased value, helping to anchor it in the construction industry without compromising its inherent socially oriented characteristics.

Using discarded earth for the production of rammed earth requires very little energy. A study on the rammed earth façade of the Ricola Kräuterzentrum calculated an 87 percent reduction in embodied energy compared to the average figures for a conventional lightweight façade, and a more than 90 percent reduction compared to a façade made of limestone.[8] Not only is the embodied energy of rammed earth low, but so are the maintenance costs of earth buildings. Rammed earth is a massive thermal material, an optimal heat sink for passive temperature regulation. The newest innovations in rammed earth, as implemented in the Alnatura project, include insulation in the prefabrication process. This allows these components to achieve industry standards in insulation and U-values while retaining earth's

Raw clay earth extracted for the Ricola Kräuterzentrum in Switzerland. Architecture by Herzog & de Meuron Architects.

The excavation pit of Haus Rauch in Austria. Architecture by Boltshauser Architekten and Martin Rauch.

Embedded hydronic pipes protrude from the prefabricated rammed earth elements of the Alnatura Arbeitswelt project in Germany. Architecture by haas cook zemmrich STUDIO2050.

Delivering gravel to the Alnatura building site in a line to prepare for the mixing.

most beneficial properties on the interior and exterior. Moreover, the thermal mass of the Alnatura project can be activated through embedded hydronic piping systems. The relative interior humidity in winter as well as summer is a pleasant 55 percent—optimal for air quality and the physical comfort of the building's occupants.[9]

Finally, constructions implemented with unstabilized earth are water-soluble, greatly simplifying their removal should such a step become necessary. It is simple to separate embedded systems and other component parts from earth and thus to recycle the material and nearly every piece of the structure. Because of these simplified processes of deconstruction, unstabilized earth can simply be folded into a new material mix and rammed again, sustaining a market without degrading the product. It would remain stable in the face of long-term impact factors such as climate change, positioning earth as a financially viable alternative for the building-materials market. As resources decrease and prices in the construction industry increase, it will make more and more financial sense for actors such as construction companies and construction-material producers such as brick-makers to invest in rammed earth construction to supplement their current products and services. As Christian Keller, owner and CEO of the Swiss brickmaking market leader Keller Ziegeleien, explained to us in a workshop about the future of construction materials, we urgently require alternatives to our current materials that use less primary energy and produce

The mixing machine developed by Lehm Ton Erde GmbH.

fewer carbon emissions.[10] Rammed earth and bricks, for example, could complement one another and open up a new market.

One means of creating more economic pressure to implement earth building is to capitalize on the potential value of prefabricating component parts. This applies both to the elements themselves, as well as to the companies that produce them. Lehm Ton Erde has recently calculated the financial impact of rammed earth of their individual projects, focusing on Central Europe, showing that revenues for rammed earth constructions primarily executed with manual labor range from between 1 and 1.5 million euros per year. With the two major innovations in prefabricated rammed earth—load-bearing modular façades and integrated insulation—five-year projections anticipate increased revenue streams of between 2 and 2.5 million euros per year for the company. The main improvements for profitability of rammed earth lie in cost reductions through technical planning and more efficient production processes.

The retail price of prefabricated rammed earth wall elements is between 1,000 and 1,200 euros per square meter, with manufacturing costs of approximately 850 and 1,000 euros per square meter. With the newest technologies and anticipated increase in use, retail prices could be expected to sink to 600 to 800 and manufacturer costs to 500 to 600 euros per square meter.[11] Modular systems with certified norms, which can seamlessly be used in combination with other materials by construction companies, represent the apex of prefabricated rammed earth's potential. When this has been achieved, the knowledge of how to design and build with rammed earth will be available to a much broader segment of the building sector.

Through prefabrication, earth is more competitive on the open market and has the potential to be financialized like conventional building materials in contexts where human labor is expensive. If we can create a roadmap for the upscaling process—meaning, if standards, expertise, material combinations, and precedent projects were to be in place, as we explore in the final chapter of this book—then earth would be well-situated to impact the existing market, catalyzing more environmentally and socially friendly processes. Considering that such "ecologized" products are increasingly coming to dominate the decision-making processes of consumers and companies alike, rammed earth could rapidly establish a market presence.

New Cross-Sectoral Alliances

While long-term change requires economic pressure, it is also tied to social demands for more healthy, sustainable, and responsible forms of development. Achieving the necessary critical mass for this change requires not only innovation across sectors but also forging new partnerships and alliances between designers, the building market, and spanning multiple segments of society. Partnerships across seemingly very different sectors can push forward alternatives to the dominance of construction materials that require fossil fuels, such as massive concrete construction.

Architects and engineers have spoken widely about the inability of the planet to sustain the trajectory of the construction industry today. Philippe Block, professor at the ETH Zurich, for example, has noted that a paradigm shift will occur in the building industry within the next three decades. "Efficiency, economy, elegance, and ecology," will be the industry's future constraints—and these will also drive innovation, he states.[12] Werner Sobek, famous for his light-construction techniques in steel and concrete, describes two possible futures for sustainable construction, which also speak directly to the benefits of earth: building for more people with less material, or immediately eliminating the use of fossil fuels in the production of materials.[13] Talking in terms of energy efficiency, Sobek argues, is the wrong approach:

> We wrap our buildings up tightly, turning them into piles of hazardous waste. We stipulate air-renewal standards and heat with

pellets, thereby happily continuing to emit CO_2 in the process. [...] There is simply no justification for this approach.[14]

Instead, he maintains, the fields of design and construction must embrace a much more radical stance: the most efficient use of materials possible. Probing the efficiency of a material without compromising its structural integrity is his personal goal in lightweight construction, in his case with concrete. This sentiment is also echoed by Philippe Block:

> We have not yet reached the point of no return, but we must find ways to design with fewer materials, to reduce structural volumes, to slow the rate at which we deplete natural resources, and to reduce or even eliminate the waste associated with construction.[15]

Some advances in reducing the use of concrete—which could potentially be combined with earth—are on the horizon within the next five to ten years.[16]

We believe that attempting to minimize fossil-fuel-based materials is a necessary and positive step. However, we also believe that reevaluating and reexploiting earth will result in a new realm of form-finding, appropriate material combinations, and architectural expression, all of which propagate social and ecological flourishing. In this sense, we advocate not only the increased

Catalan vaulting by the Block Research Group at the Venice Architecture Biennale (2016). Thin-tile vaulting serves as a means of maxmizing the potential of materials for sustainable construction.

Another form of material maximizing developed by the Block Research Group to digitally fabricate thin concrete components.

use of earth but also the most efficient use possible of high-carbon-footprint materials such as concrete. There is potential to forge an alliance around the principles of extreme efficiency in design and a rejection of fossil fuels and no reason why, in the right context, lightweight and massive constructions cannot complement one another. In this way, unexpected alliances could begin to engender gradual change in building practices, through research and high-quality built projects.

New Social Objectives

Whether artistically, constructively, or through the material itself, the endeavor of sustainable building should always be coupled with a social objective and underpinned by broad political support. In related discussions on climate change, policy advocate Ted Halstead, for example, notes that the barriers to progress are threefold: psychological, geopolitical, and partisan.[17] People are fearful and skeptical of change, certain geographical locations are more impacted than others, and political parties prefer to maintain the status quo for their voters and (more important) their donors. What underlies the kind of action required to address climate change is a sense for the common good, an attitude that we must embrace what is best for everyone rather than just ourselves.[18] As the impact of climate change becomes more tangible, conceiving systems to control the negative externalities of the building industry is one of the most crucial steps toward long-term sustainability.

The Climate Leadership Council in the United States is an example of an unexpected alliance of politically conservative individuals who believe in the urgency of addressing climate change and that it should be driven by the private sector. This council is convinced that once financial feasibility is taken out of the equation, companies and people can be trusted to make choices to reduce emissions and purchase products that impact the environment less. They promote implementing a carbon tax, which would begin at a low level and be raised incrementally. Most important, they propose is that the dividends from this tax would not go to the U.S. government but would be redistributed to American families. They calculate that, for example, were a carbon tax of 40 USD per ton of cement to be imposed, 2,000 USD per year could be given back to more than 225 million people, which would more than cover the energy expenses for these families.[19]

While market-oriented solutions like a carbon tax cannot alone solve the urgent problems of climate change, these kinds of objectives—not just environmental and economic, but also social—are well-aligned with the kind of unstabilized and fully recyclable earth building we advocate. Consider the implications for the housing market were more houses to be built with earth and even potentially constructed directly from their site of excavation. The threshold for simple constructions of earth would be lower, making the production of a home much more accessible to a large sector of the global population. Scholars such as the German-American lawyer and urbanist Peter Marcuse assert that changes making the housing market more accessible even have the potential to make our societies more equitable—preventing future market collapses and worldwide recessions.[20] This could shift the perception of a home as a financialized object. Rather than as an investment to be continually maintained for the purposes of buying and selling (representing a commodification of land and life), investment would be directed toward its component parts—its heating and cooling systems, its appliances, its furnishings—that can be removed and resold on a microscale. The cycles of production and consumption required for upkeep and maintenance of materials that have a higher environmental impact, degrade with time and use, and must always be "downscaled" could gradually be destabilized.

On a local and personal level, earth also connects and sustains people. Part of its power is in the recognition that our lives and our constructions are ephemeral and should be created collectively. Embracing the thick walls of a massive construction, when appropriate, executing material combinations to achieve maximum efficiency, and finding a balance between the power of human labor and the suitable application of technology is the backbone of our philosophy for sustainable building. This also speaks directly to the material, process, and catalyst nature of earth—coming together to create a small resource footprint through maximizing local materials, manpower, and craftsmanship.

Building a Community

A.H. Finding a balance between labor and technology in the European context does not inherently mean a high degree of technology. It also represents an increased emphasis on participation, in an attempt to get more people involved in shaping the surrounding environment and embracing the archaic power of building with earth. Earth is also a mythical substance, the center of creation stories from indigenous practices to mainstream Christianity.

Our project in the Worms Cathedral embodies this myth of earth as a substance of unity and creation. To celebrate the one-thousand-year anniversary of the basilica of St. Peter's in Worms, the parish announced a competition to redesign the sanctuary surrounding the altar. This cathedral is a masterpiece of Romanesque architecture, with a Baroque interior.

While in the Baroque period, gold and other opulent materials were utilized to represent the beauty and wealth of creation, the design by our team, Heringer & Rauch, focused instead on the simplicity of earth. The central element of the project is the altar—a symbol of Christianity and also a symbolic coming together of the local community between Heaven and Earth. To focus the dynamic space of the cathedral onto this *axis mundi* of the sanctuary, the design of the liturgical elements was conducted with restraint. The modesty of earth brings the concepts of holiness and peace to life like no other material. It also encapsulates unparalleled authenticity: its beauty lies in its simplicity. The traces of the process of construction—the human energy stamped into the material—remain visible on the surface of its elements, in its manifold layers. And, in the spirit of celebrating the power of human labor and a living community, members of the parish produced the altar by hand.

Construction of the project commenced in summer 2018. It fully embraces the principles of Pope Francis's second encyclical,

Laudato Si, critiquing blatant consumerism and irresponsible development practices, while highlighting the dangers of environmental degradation and the threat of global warming.[21] This letter calls all people of the world to take "swift and unified global action" in the face of these urgent challenges, not just in an environmental sense but also in regard to socially ethical practices and a conscious responsibility as stewards of the planet.[22]

One of the most poignant learning experiences from my time in Bangladesh was discovering that architecture is not just about putting up walls but about building a community. In years past, people came together to build a chapel, or a mosque, or a school, or city hall. These acts were fundamentally associative, foundational to the idea of community in the first place. As French writer Antoine de Saint-Exupéry noted in *Wisdom of the Sands*: "If you wish them to be brothers, have them build a tower. But if you would have them hate each other, throw them corn."[23] Interpreting this, mere objects do not have meaning in themselves—it is

Volunteers in the Worms Cathedral hand-ramming the altar by Anna Heringer and Martin Rauch.

Removing the formwork from the altar in Worms. Church members executed the ramming process themselves.

Detail of the altar's corner.

the meaning we ascribe to them that matters. Community lives through shared aspirations and concrete tasks, rather than simple provision of resources. This axiom is as relevant in a context with infinite resources as it is in one with very few.

1   Erika Bellmann and Patrick Zimmermann, *Climate Protection in the Concrete and Cement Industry : Background and Possible Courses of Action* (Berlin: WWF Germany, 2019), p. 10.
2   Ibid. pp. 10–24
3   Interview with Dirk Hebel (November 30, 2021).
4   Bellmann and Zimmermann, p. 24 (see note 1)
5   Ibid., pp. 21–22
6   Dirk Hebel (see note 3)
7   Katharina Edinger, "Das Haus von morgen, Wie Bauen revolutioniert wird," *plan b*, ZDF (first broadcast September 9, 2018), https://www.youtube.com/watch?v=uh7JJU1LgP0&ab_channel=UpscalingEarth (accessed December 23, 2018), 26:20 and 27:00.
8   Lehm Ton Erde "Vorgefertigte, tragende Systembauweise aus nicht stabilisiertem Stampflehm," unpublished research application to the Österreichische Forschungsförderungsgesellschaft und Vorarlberger Landesregierung (October 10, 2017), p. 16.
9   Calculations into the embodied energy required for the Alnatura Arbeitswelt project are currently in the process of being compiled with a grant from the German Federal Environmental Foundation and as a joint venture between the builders Campus 360 GmbH, architects haas cook zemmrich STUDIO2050, climate engineers Transsolar, and the Technical University of Munich.
10   Workshop with Christian Keller, Jürgen Laartz, Veronika Darius, Martin Rauch, and Anna Heringer (November 30, 2016).

11   Lehm Ton Erde, "Vorgefertigte, tragende Systembauweise," p. 29 (see note 2).
12   Philippe Block and Noelle Paulson, "E4: Efficiency, Economy, Elegance, and Ecology," in *Design—Tales of Science and Innovation* (Zurich: G. Folkers and M. Schmid, Chronos Verlag, Collegium Helveticum, and ETH Zurich, 2019), pp. 1–3, here p. 1.
13   Werner Sobek, as cited in interview with Jenny Keller, "Lösung für die gebaute Welt von Morgen," *Swiss-Architects Magazine,* May 24, 2018, https://www.swiss-architects.com/de/architecture-news/hintergrund/loesungen-fuer-die-gebaute-welt-von-morgen (accessed September 14, 2018).
14   Ibid.
15   Block and Paulson, "E4," p. 1 (see note 6). See also John Orr, Michal Drewniok, Ian Walkerb, Tim Ibellc, Alexander Copping, and Stephen Emmitt, "Minimising Energy in Construction: Practitioners' Views on Material Efficiency," *Resources, Conservation & Recycling* 140 (2019), pp. 125–136.
16   For example, the Karlsruhe Institute of Technology is developing a process to fabricate cement at 400 degrees Celsius rather than 1,800 degrees Celsius, which would result in significant energy savings and reduced fossil fuel use. Another initiative proposes replacing steel reinforcement in concrete construction with carbon webbing, reducing the amount of cement required by nearly 50 percent. This, however, is an extremely expensive process. See Judith Schneider, "Zement—der heimliche Klimakiller," *Planet-E*, ZDF (first broadcast May 5, 2018), https://www.zdf.de/dokumentation/planet-e/planet-e-zement---der-heimliche-klimakiller-100.html (accessed September 14, 2018), 21:41 and 23:00.
17   Ted Halstead, "A Climate Solution Where All Sides Can Win," *TED Talk*, TED Annual Conference, Vancouver, British Columbia (April 2017), https://www.ted.com/talks/ted_halstead_a_climate_solution_where_all_sides_can_win (accessed September 14, 2018).
18   See Elinor Ostrom, *Governing the Commons: The Evolution of Institutions for Collective Action* (Cambridge: Cambridge University Press, 1990).
19   Halstead, "Climate Solution" (see note 11).
20   Peter Marcuse, "Whose Right(s) to What City?" in Neil Brenner, Peter Marcuse, and Margit Mayer (eds.), *Cities for People, Not for Profit: Critical Urban Theory and the Right to the City* (New York: Routledge, 2009), pp. 24–41.
21   Pope Francis, *Laudato Si of the Holy Father Francis: On Care for Our Common Home*, encyclical letter (Vatican City: Libreria Editrice Vaticana, 2015), http://w2.vatican.va/content/francesco/en/encyclicals/documents/papa-francesco_20150524_enciclica-laudato-si.html (accessed September 14, 2018).
22   Jim Yardley and Laurie Goodstein, "Pope Francis, in Sweeping Encyclical, Calls for Swift Action on Climate Change," *New York Times,* June 18, 2015.
23   Antoine de Saint-Exupéry, *Wisdom of the Sands* (Chicago: University of Chicago Press, 1979), p. 52.

A Roadmap for Upscaling

Advocating earth building represents a stance against the overuse of materials with high environmental impacts and low social returns. The point is not to replace all other materials, such as concrete, with earth, but to use such high-carbon-footprint materials appropriately and in moderation. Earth is an extremely valuable alternative, at the interstice of responsible development and technological advancement. Upscaling earth aims to invest in and return knowledge to local communities by means of local resources.

The two most important prerequisites for upscaling earth building are: (1) overcoming the fears associated with the material itself, and (2) creating a roadmap of what must be done to advance its common use. The primary apprehensions impeding the use of earth in highly industrialized contexts relate to its perceived vulnerability and the labor-intensive implementation process involved. To address these fears, the process of building with earth must be normed, and experts in designing and building with earth have to be trained. Then, trust in the material must be strengthened through distinctive flagship projects. Once norms, experts, and built works are established, a framework could be articulated with which bids for earthen construction could then be tendered—such as publicly funded projects—thus precipitating upscaling. While these are institutional strategies, the actions each and every one of us takes can also impact how the world around us is shaped. We therefore conclude with the outline of a potential trajectory for the future of earth as a material, process, and catalyst, with people at the center.

Overcoming Fears

The socio-technical goal of upscaling earth is to advance its use in design globally. However, materials also have the power to catalyze new movements with far-reaching ramifications. For example, modernism was a movement in architecture tied to material advancements in building with concrete and steel and glass. Earth, too, has this power, particularly as pressing environmental problems are compounded by highly technical building requirements.

But there is a lack of trust in the material earth, which we believe exists due to a lack of knowledge about the process of how to construct modern buildings in earth. The standard qualms surrounding the use of earth are: (1) it erodes; (2) it cannot bear loads, especially in earthquake zones; and (3) it cannot meet the aesthetic and practical requirements of contemporary building. Critics assert it simply cannot be implemented on modern construction sites, where all of the various subcontractors must be intricately planned and timed.

In response to the first assertion: it is true that earth is vulnerable to a certain extent. It is not eternal, in part because it is water-soluble. The primary threat to an earthen façade is running water, whether from driving rain or runoff, and historical constructions in earth typically deployed large roof overhangs to protect the walls. This is not a particularly modern aesthetic and is part of the reason many contemporary architects *stabilize* earthen constructions with cement, lime, bitumen, or silicon. However, rather than destroying earth's most beneficial properties through stabilization, or resigning oneself to other construction materials, designs can respond to the characteristics of the material by designing according to the principle of calculated erosion, as elaborated in our discussion of the material properties and potentials of rammed earth earlier in this book.

The second criticism of earth as a building material is that it cannot safely and adequately bear loads, especially if subjected to earthquakes. This misconception persists despite a large body of lab testing and published standards for its material properties.[1] The relationship between material strength and the compressive strength of rammed earth elements, for example, has been tested extensively.[2] Nevertheless, what most significantly impedes the public perception of earth building is relatively clear: vernacular earth buildings are predominantly erected by people with insufficient experience in earth building, or in any form of construction at all. Although this includes countries where building with earth is a traditional practice, the knowledge of designing to suit this material has often been lost. This phenomenon is particularly troublesome in earthquake zones. For example, when people with no training build with earth in under-resourced contexts, they often combine walls of earth with ceilings of corrugated metal sheeting affixed with rocks and loose earth or use heavy timber beams to support a roof system. This became evident, for instance, in Iran in 2003 and in Turkey in 2011, when earthquakes resulted in the deaths of many underprivileged *gecekondu* neighborhood residents.[3] Instead of addressing the specific problem by providing education to underprivileged inhabitants as to how to build safely with the materials they possess, the Turkish government responded by passing a law forbidding building with earth.

This example illustrates the general problem in upscaling earth: one must design *with* the material, and this material is simply not well understood. In regard to its behavior when subjected to earthquake loading, not just its compressive strength but also its shear strength is important. The compressive strength of concrete, for example, is 12.5 newtons per square millimeter while that of rammed earth is 2.4 newtons per square millimeter.[4] However, rammed earth can absorb considerably more lateral load, and in zones subject to regular or intensive earthquake loading, can be used in combination with a primary structural system of steel. This kind of material combination is a more appropriate solution, despite stigmas that suggest otherwise. As a final benefit, if damage occurs during an earthquake, components can be significantly more easily repaired or replaced than their counterparts in concrete.

The third and final most common misperception of earth is that it cannot meet the standards of our urbanized world and high-tech building culture. Walls built with earth are simply too thick, many designers assert, and it cannot be used for ceilings and floors. The projects cataloged in this publication all serve as solid evidence refuting these claims—as well as the claim that progress in earth building should be explored on a material level, through stabilization. Thick walls should be embraced where appropriate—for example in contexts requiring thermal mass for passive heating and cooling, and in which moisture can be exchanged between a building's materials and its occupants. Haus Rauch, for instance, functions according to this concept: an approach to design grounded in the sustainable material combination of earth and timber.[5] "Why shouldn't we have thick walls when the material is for free?" notes Matthias Schuler of the climate-engineering firm Transsolar. "We must learn to think in terms of comfort rather than [holding fast to] our range of 18–22 degrees of interior temperatures, which do not even incorporate moisture vapor!" he asserts.[6]

House M. in Rankweil, Austria (1993–1996). A combination of tile and trass-lime speed breakers has allowed the façade to withstand weathering in Vorarlberg for decades. Architecture by Robert Felber and Martin Rauch.

It is also important that building with earth is feasible according to the timelines and normative standards of contemporary building sites. The prefabrication of rammed earth components makes it possible to separate the production process from the site, instead of constructing in situ as is common in traditional earth building. Today, it is possible to achieve a 3:1 ratio between the time required to prefabricate rammed earth components and the time required to set them in place on a building site, significantly reducing labor costs in industrialized contexts.

Rammed earth possesses a strikingly modern aesthetic while retaining an archaic connection to our planet and expressing a unique identity for each place and project. What matters the most is the quality of spaces—in a physical and phenomenological sense—and the traces their construction leaves behind. Throughout human history, combining earth with other building materials has resulted in beautiful, durable, and appropriate structures that closed building systems simply cannot achieve.

Norms, Research, and Education

Upscaling earth is not just a discussion among architecture and building-industry practitioners. Even international consultants and large conglomerates such as brick manufacturers are beginning to explore the possibility that the industry will experience significant change in the coming decades. To understand the perspective of the private sector, we conducted a workshop with retired McKinsey senior partner Jürgen Laartz and Keller Ziegeleien owner and CEO Christian Keller. We discussed the necessary prerequisites for earthen construction—in particular for rammed earth—in order for it to become more widely used in both fully industrialized as well as emerging economies.[7] Ultimately, both Laartz and Keller asserted, materials that rely on fossil fuels such as concrete and fired bricks will become extremely expensive for the consumer. If today's conventions continue, they conceded, the initial investment in resources and capital and the amortization and maintenance of buildings will simply become unaffordable. And taking the environmental ethics or social responsibility of fossil fuels—their true costs—into account provides even more incentive to turn our focus to materials like earth.[8]

Earth building in earthquake zones must be conducted with particular care, especially in regard to roof constructions with loose earth. Education is an extremely important aspect of upscaling earthen architecture, as is the incorporation of appropriate technologies.

Earth could fill this void if two things occur: there is a commonly accepted procedure for its implementation and there are enough technical experts who can design with earth and lead its construction. Building with earth must become faster, easier, and less risky. What currently precludes innovation with earth more than any other aspect is a lack of precedents and experiences to create standards for planning large-scale projects. We are thoroughly convinced that innovation will begin to flourish once a set of rules for building with earth is established and trained experts become more widely available.

The first target for elevating earth and edifying its process is to establish rules that are capable of incorporating both variances in the material itself as well as variances in cultural practices. The purpose of norms is to cre-

Material combinations can provide structural stability and a contemporary aesthetic for any project, as shown with the round window in the Ricola Kräuterzentrum project by Herzog & de Meuron Architects.

ate safe, replicable solutions for implementing large-scale projects—but without destroying the emancipatory aspects of working with earth locally. For this reason, we deliberately emphasize targeting the process of earthen construction as well as the necessity of certifying practitioners. If there were a standardized set of rules as to how this process can occur across a range of conditions, and if it included certified experts to oversee the building sites and monitor quality, the production of earthen elements would become both marketable and purchasable on a larger scale.

Codifying these rules into more formalized norms should enable finding a balance between static rules and local challenges. This requires an initial decision about what should be normed in the first place. For example, with rammed earth, the questions would be: What standards for the material are essential to ensure safety regardless of the manufacturing process? How can technical specifications and the quality of the material mixture be guaranteed? Which aspects of the prefabrication process can be standardized, and how can this be determined?

To begin this process, rammed earth needs to be thoroughly tested and evaluated on a material level. The physical properties of shrinkage and elasticity in the clay, the sheer strength of material mixtures, and the impact of frost and moisture on rammed earth elements all require further technical investigation. Then, a range of acceptable values for compressive strength, as well as safety factors with respect to static loads, live loads, and earthquake loading must be established. To achieve these targets, the process of finding the correct mixture must then be specified: a ratio of clay and supplementary natural materials such as gravel, sand, or fibers like straw that can be adapted to each local context. Prototypes can then be produced according to these specifications, and subjected to another round of testing and evaluation, including, for example, cavity walls with integrated insulation as in Lehm Ton Erde's walls for the Alnatura Arbeitswelt project in Darmstadt. In short, applied research is fundamental to developing further such innovations.

Once quality-related criteria are established, norming can proceed by forming an interest group composed of a wide range of stakeholders. This group, usually comprising seven participants, could include architects, building-materials experts, and structural engineers. Once this group agrees on a set of norms, which is of course a complex and time-consuming endeavor, they can be certified and implemented. This is important for upscaling, because in many countries taxpayer-financed government projects are only permissible once certified norms for a material have been established. Then, according to Jürgen Laartz, the normed process requires a marketing strategy: brand recognition for a product is extremely important, both for issuing calls for tender as well as giving companies the confidence to assume liability for earthen products.[9]

As noted by climate-disaster specialist Garry de la Pomerai at a 2016 environmental risk management symposium in Davos, materials like earth are often banned by governments, regardless of their incredible potential, because they lack internationally defined norms. Instead, it remains easier to build with normed materials such as concrete, even though we have yet to

ETH Zurich students at Studio Heringer-Rauch participating in a Claystorming exercise.

Anna Heringer and Martin Rauch built the MudWorks Wall (2012) at the Harvard Graduate School of Design, creating a social space with this warm, tactile installation.

fully grasp their impact on climate or how our practices will shift as the climate inevitably changes. As de la Pomerai explains:

> It's easier to ban [earth] than to understand it. Yet we [must] react to climate change and create resilience for climate change. It's not necessarily reacting to floods and tsunamis, it's temperature change. We've had a comfort zone in these climates over the past several hundred years and these things are going to change. We don't know how it's going to alter, but we do know that traditional methods have been resilient to the extremes of summers, extremes of winters, hot and colds, whereas we're not sure about concrete yet. We're still discovering its limitations.[10]

Therefore, part of the second target for upscaling earth is increasing expertise in how to build with unstabilized earth, encompassing architectural design, technical production, and exploratory research such that it becomes adequately established for the authorities who have the power to grant or deny building projects. Currently, building with earth is a proverbial catch-22: training in the art of earth building requires experts, yet due to a lack of teachers to educate future experts they remain few and far between. Moreover, earth continues to be perceived as an exotic product for a niche market, meaning that there are a limited number of craftsmen or artisans who specialize in this kind of earthen architecture today to lead unskilled laborers, while large production facilities that could potentially compensate for this lack remain practically nonexistent.

For there to be more technical experts able to supervise the execution of earth building, we ourselves are convinced that it must become a part of educational curriculums, involving workshops, collaborative academic investigations, and networks for craftsmen and engineers and architects. Part of our mission is to excite the next generation of architects and designers about building with unstabilized earth, as we have done at institutions including the Harvard Graduate School of Design, ETH Zurich, University of Liechtenstein, Technical University of Munich, Technical University of Vienna, and University of Linz.

Demonstrating Upscaling

Our early experiences with design-build projects arose from a deep and indelible connection to earth itself. It is not a coincidence that all three of us first came into contact with earth in under-resourced and underprivileged contexts—in Tanzania, Bangladesh, and Ethiopia—where we each directly encountered the great potential of earth to act as a catalyst, experiencing the hands-on praxis and spirit of collaboration that underlies best-practice projects.

During our time at the ETH Zurich, we aimed to provide a similarly transformative experience for our students, in particular through the design-build studio we executed in Mdabulo, Tanzania. Our teaching team included the architects Christian Schmitt and Wayne Switzer, who also developed the technical planning and implementation of the project. In the studio, the five of us worked closely with local NGO partners the Rural Development Organization (RDO) and Eine Welt Gruppe Schlins to devise the design brief. Aligned with our metric for successful development cooperation projects, we attempted to work appropriately, delivering not only a product and a process but equally a catalyst for further development. The intention was to provide the students with an opportunity to engage with the challenge of

Studio Heringer-Rauch students from the ETH Zurich discuss their designs for orphan housing and a community center with Hannes Rauch, representative of the NGO "Eine Welt Gruppe" in Mdabulo, Tanzania.

Summer school participants constructed two homes for orphans along with members of the local community in 2015. Communicating through models was essential to the design and construction process.

designing with few resources, as well as a chance for them to question both the roll of the architect in a globalized world and the underlying nature of what is commonly labeled "development work."

Due to the fact that several members of the Rauch family had been involved in the Mdabulo region for decades, we were able to root the design brief in comprehensive knowledge of the place and its people. The project involved designing a community center and two prototype houses for orphans. According to the World Bank, nearly 45 percent of Tanzania's inhabitants are under fifteen years of age, and HIV is extremely widespread.[11] Because of its traditional system of inheritance, orphans whose parents have died of AIDS often remain in their parents' home in the same village but have no means of supporting themselves. The new houses were conceived as two durable, simply built rammed earth buildings, executed using local materials so that the local population could be trained in the techniques of construction. Through this, we aimed not just to provide a durable space for orphaned children but to also establish a framework for the replication of the building process, creating a positive, lasting impact on the building culture of the village. The community center included a large assembly space and smaller functional areas, such as a kitchen and workshop, and at the same time represented the chance to upscale the skills and techniques utilized for the houses.

The site was located in the highlands of Tanzania, where temperatures regularly oscillate between very hot days and very cold nights. Massive construction is therefore well-suited to the local climate. Moreover, ramming earth had actually been a traditional building method in the area, but the knowledge of how to execute it correctly, in a durable manner, had been lost over the past several generations. In the meantime, adobe bricks had persisted, but those who could afford the high cost of concrete blocks had used them as a substitute for earth—although this remained rare in the remote village. Phidelis, our client at the RDO in Mdabulo as well as the project manager on the site, told us how his father had built a "modern" concrete-block house several years previously, but how, because it was much too hot in the summer and much too cold in the winter after the sun set, the family always returned to their earth house when they wanted to sleep at night.

The project comprised one design semester at the ETH Zurich and a summer school for the implementation of the selected designs. Our team juried

A Roadmap for Upscaling

Floor plan for House Ajeli, the larger of two homes constructed in Mdabulo.

Formwork for rammed earth encases Ajeli's exterior walls, while the interior walls with an integrated chimney and niches are complete.

House Ajeli three years after completing construction.

The interior rammed earth wall of House Ajeli was finished with brightly colored earth plastering and its roof constructed with woven reed mats.

Floor plan for House Shangwe, the smaller of two homes constructed in Mdabulo.

House Shangwe from the rear, with three small windows, three years after completing construction.

The front of House Shangwe with its integrated niche.

each student design after final reviews with a representative from the local NGO, selecting houses by two students and a community center designed by a group of seven students. We also worked collaboratively with several other partners at the ETH Zurich throughout the project: Philippe Block and his assistants Marcel Aubert and Patrik Meyer; Jan Carmeliet and Kristina Orehousing; and several master's students at Carmeliet's Chair for Integrated Building Systems, who contributed to the climatic design through modeling and simulations. Twenty-five ETH students participated in the design semester, and forty students from the ETH and other institutions participated in the summer school. Architect Karolina Szulc-Switzer co-managed the building site and coordinated the students, together with Wayne Switzer.

Several aspects of the project represented an upscaling of earth. In Mdabulo, rammed earth proved to be a particularly appropriate building technique because local people had already collected quantities of small stones and gravel from the nearby fields to create earthen mixtures for adobe bricks.

A Roadmap for Upscaling

Thirty to forty percent of the earth mixture for this project was composed of such stones, so the process of breaking them into the correct size became one of the first ways that the project was able to generate income for the villagers. We sought to impart the importance of creating the correct mixture, as well as protecting the rammed earth walls with reinforced stone foundations and appropriate roofing, emphasizing both the material and the process. We also took advantage of one of the recent changes to the agricultural system in the area to experiment with a lighter typology of earthen elements. Over the past twenty years, many pine-tree forests had grown, so that fallen pine needles often covered the ground up to 15 centimeters deep. These shed needles acidify the soil as they decompose, but they could also be collected and used as reinforcement in the earth mixture, yielding a lighter substance and better insulation values. An easy-to-use innovation, it has already begun to be subsequently replicated in Mdabulo to improve the quality of traditional adobe bricks.

Quarry where gravel was sourced for the project in Mdabulo, acting as a catalyst for further development.

AJELI

SHANGWE

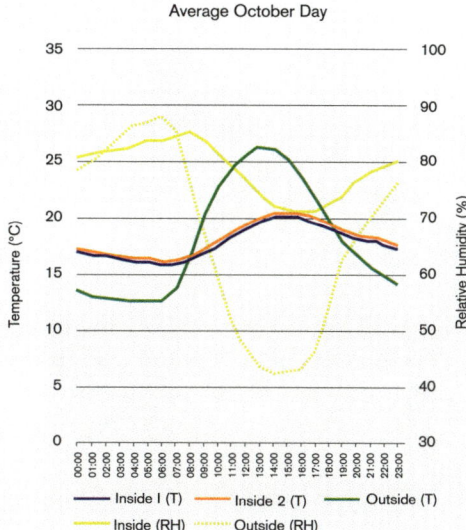

EXISTING HOUSE

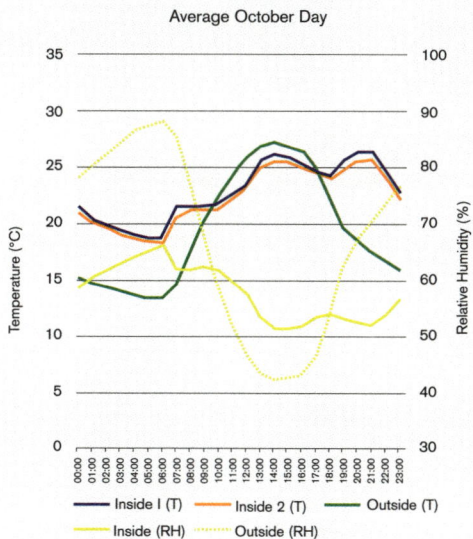

Comparison of climate conditions in Ajeli and Shangwe houses with a preexisting earthen house on an average October day in 2016.

A Roadmap for Upscaling

Construction of the community center began during the summer school in 2015 and was initially halted due to budget constraints. It continued during two subsequent dry seasons thereafter.

The Mdabulo Community Center in 2017, as construction recommenced, allowed village residents to learn skills which were then transferred to the construction of a prefabricated rammed earth wall for the Swiss Embassy in Dar es Salaam.

Floor plan for the Mdabulo Community Center, conceived by Studio Heringer-Rauch students.

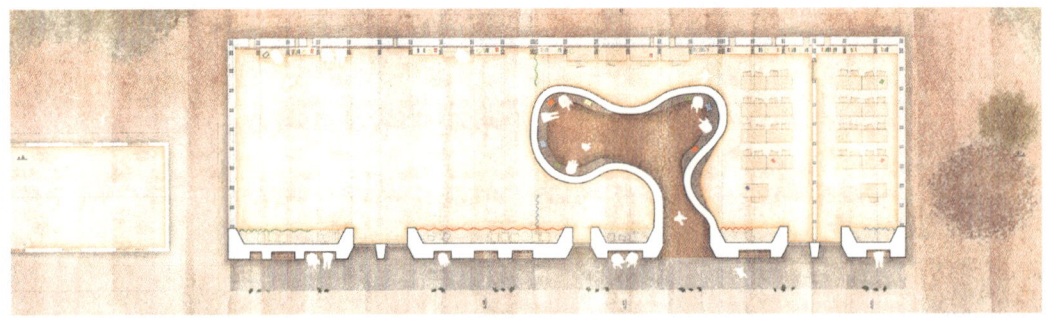

Women of Mdabulo plastering the façade of the community center, which is generating income for the village and continuing to catalyze socially just development.

Knowledge transfer is one of the most important potentials of upscaling earth, not just because it becomes embedded incrementally in building cultures, but because it has ramifications that can create long-term socio-economic opportunities. The community center in Mdabulo is now a highly sought-after venue, generating significant income for the village through rentals and serving as a catalyst for further sustainable and socially oriented building. Over the past two years since the two houses were completed, we have noticed that more and more villagers have begun to build with unreinforced earth. Furthermore, some of the local craftsmen we trained have begun to produce rammed earth elements for other, larger-scale projects. Via

Gunter Klix of the Lucerne University of Applied Sciences and Arts, our work in Mdabulo came to the attention of the Swiss ambassador in Dar es Salaam. The embassy wanted to renovate their facilities in rammed earth but could not find any technical experts in Tanzania's former capital. The solution was that the people our team had previously trained in Mdabulo prefabricated the wall in their village, cut it down into component parts, and transported them to Dar es Salaam, where they were then reassembled and retouched to form the wall. Especially when considering the legacy of embassy building in Africa, and across the former colonies of the world, which relied on imported and expensive materials, building this wall was both a sustainable constructive decision and a symbolic gesture. Recognizing the value of local materials and the social impact of building reflects a consciousness that we as designers must urgently embrace.

In Mdabulo, at first people were highly skeptical about how to design with earth. But they were fascinated by its aesthetics, by its haptic qualities, and by its archaic nature. It is this visual aesthetic of earth that has also begun to entrance architects and designers worldwide. While laudable, there is a danger that this aesthetic will be copied, but not the social impact or environmental benefits of the substance itself. This faux usage includes changing the physical properties of earth through chemical additives and stabilization, when in fact earth should remain unchanged as much as possible, so that it can be fully recycled.

We would argue that it is imperative that decision-making figures and educational institutions understand why earth is so beneficial. Integrating it into teaching would, in turn, magnify upscaling in the long-term. Basic and applied research must also be conducted at university level to ensure that investigations into the physical possibilities of the material and an optimization of its processes are driven forward. There have been some exciting and groundbreaking initiatives investigating the stabilization of earth at the ETH Zurich, in particular the work of Guillaume Habert and Gnanli Landrou into "pouring" earth-like concrete by supplementing earth with cementitious binding agents.[12] Funding must be secured for research into untreated and fully recyclable unstabilized earth as well.

To summarize these arguments: Without the development of norms and an increase in trained professionals, this roadmap we are outlining for upscaling is unlikely to occur. Current national laws—for instance, in Germany, Italy,

Turkey, or Colombia—are so preventative as to stifle material and process innovations in earth building. There remains a dearth of pilot projects and of publications, a limited presence in the media, and an underrepresentation in educational curricula, which impedes training skilled laborers to realize innovative projects. As American architect and urbanist Michael Sorkin has written:

> In order to secure a sustainable future, we need enormous investment in research and education. This will not simply be to invent the new technologies to enable a more sustainable future—including that gamut that surrounds building and fabrication—but to create generations of citizens who know the value of living in harmony with the planet's rhythms and resources and who have had the practices of sharing and generosity imbued in them.[13]

This philosophy is encapsulated in building with earth the material, earth the process, and earth the catalyst.

Let us try to imagine scenarios in which earth building could begin to foster change on a greater scale. Cities or municipalities could begin to invest in the machinery to fabricate earthen elements for construction, subsidizing construction that could directly involve people and communities. One would require only the necessary skills to operate the machinery and ensure that the produced elements meet building-material and site standards. Through this, reliance on external corporations to supply expensive materials and oversee construction processes could be significantly reduced. While this principle could apply, in theory, to any building material, earth is the most sustainable and renewable alternative that is suited to socially driven objectives. As such, the topic is even beginning to take root in public consciousness, even if only in a precursory fashion: Tesla CEO Elon Musk tweeted—since tweets seem to count as discussion, or even as presidential decrees in our current era—the possibility of utilizing the material unearthed by his tunnel-digging company to create bricks for low-cost housing in Los Angeles.[14] If urban areas—in particular, underprivileged areas—could access the simple technology and material to create rammed elements, for example, it would provide cities with great flexibility and resilience to meet the needs of their current and future inhabitants.

We Are the Lobby!

Upscaling means change. Upscaling means establishing earth as a convention in our contemporary building culture—through technical norms and socially oriented processes. Once norms and education are secured, the prerequisites for upscaling will be in place. However, these changes will most likely require support from our political institutions. It is the political process that allots financing for research and education and that legitimizes accepted norms, meaning that any progress without institutional support would be even more challenging. Therefore our mission has to be to convince government bodies to institutionalize its use by strongly formulating our vision of what it means to build with earth. As Farrokh Derakhshani, director of the Aga Khan Award for Architecture, has stated:

> Mud, besides water, is one of the most precious materials in the service of mankind. Food is cultivated on it, it absorbs CO_2 when greenery is grown on it, and it is used to create shelter. Best of all, once it is used for any of these purposes, it gets recycled back.[15]

Particularly in the future—with increasing social, economic, and environmental costs for construction—a conscious choice of construction materials, and an understanding of their environmental, economic, and social impact will be crucial for each and every building project.

At the beginning of this book we posed several questions that underlie the future of our building culture, with its intricately interconnected global and local aspects: How do we want to live? What are our dreams for how we shape the world around us? Where do these images come from, and how can we move from our current realities toward these visions?

Our collective answer is that we—regardless of hemisphere, or level of privilege, or access to resources—want to live in a world made for both current and future generations, not one which exploits our environmental and social systems for profit. This world has a strong sense of identity, and this includes the cultural ideal of building so as to develop structures true to their materials and responsive to people's needs. To be sustainable, we must live in harmony with nature to the greatest degree possible. This means accepting creation and decay, focusing on constructing a building based on its optimal life cycle and maximum participation rather than seeking to build objects with fossil-fuel-based materials and a maximum return on interest. To achieve this kind of world, we must exercise our collective rights as residents of the planet to reorient building practices toward these objectives. Any truly meaningful common goal must be twofold: jettisoning fossil fuels and creating materials and processes that act as catalysts.

As the problems of our building cultures become relevant to the private sector (for whom they pose both great financial risks and opportunities), and to individual members of society (who must bear their impact), people and economies have the power to engender change. However, in the end, this change must be codified through politics. There are numerous emerging movements seeking to "ecologize" the economy and that extol the virtue of the common good—objectives with which building with earth is perfectly aligned. However, upscaling earth can only be successful if there are enough designers, decision-makers, and enterprises that can build with earth.

As this book aims to show, this is neither a utopian ideal nor some sort of "return to the Stone Age" by propagating backward construction methods. Earth as a material, as a process, and as a catalyst is more like the "experimental utopias" conceived by the philosopher and urbanist Henri Lefebvre, who stated that "in order to extend the possible, it is necessary to proclaim and desire the impossible. Action and strategy consist in making possible tomorrow what is impossible today." [16] We ourselves have a vision for the future we want and have traced an outline of how we can achieve an upscaling of building and constructing with earth. Refining this plan will require much more collaboration, many more projects, and a great deal of passion. We hope this book provides an impetus and inspiration to pursue a more sustainable and conscientious common future in building practices. Together, we can reconstitute what is possible.

Hence this call to arms for all those who seek to shape the world around them: We are the lobby! It is our stance, our actions, and our choices of means that will determine whether our dreams for the world around us become reality. Earth can play a key role in a more sustainable future. We, too, can become catalysts for change.

1   See Dachverband Lehm (ed.), *Lehmbau Regeln: Begriffe Baustoffe Bauteile* (Wiesbaden: Vieweg+Teubner, 2002), pp. 6–10.
2   See Gernot Minke, *Building with Earth: Design and Technology of a Sustainable Architecture* (Basel: Birkhäuser, 2012, 3rd ed.), pp. 32–33.
3   Gecekondu is a culturally specific form of unregulated urban settlement in Turkey. See Ozan Karaman, "Urban Renewal in Istanbul: Reconfigured Spaces, Robotic Lives," *International Journal of Urban and Regional Research* 37, no. 2 (2013), pp. 715–33, here pp. 718–19.
4   Newtons per millimeter squared, also known as a megapascal. This unit describes the amount of pressure a material can withstand in stress testing, with higher values indicating more capacity to withstand stress.
5   Roger Boltshauser and Martin Rauch, *Haus Rauch/The Rauch House: Ein Modell moderner Lehmarchitektur/A Model of Advanced Clay Architecture* (Basel: Birkhäuser, 2011); Marco Sauer and Otto Kapfinger (eds.), *Martin Rauch: Refined Earth — Construction & Design with Rammed Earth* (Munich: Edition DETAIL, 2016).
6   Matthias Schuler, workshop in La Donaira, Spain (July 27, 2018).
7   Workshop with Christian Keller, Jürgen Laartz, Veronika Darius, Martin Rauch, and Anna Heringer (November 30, 2016).
8   See also Axel Simon, "Zukünftige Ziegel," in "Hochparterre," special issue, Lehmliebe, September 2018, pp. 14–23.
9   Keller and Laartz, workshop (see note 7).
10 Garry de la Pomerai, speaking at "Session 29: Towards a Resilient Built Environment" at the 6th International Disaster and Risk Conference, Davos (August 31, 2016).
11 "Population Ages 0–14 (% of Total)," in World Bank, *The World Bank IBRD IDA Data*, https://data.worldbank.org/indicator/SP.POP.0014.TO.ZS?locations=TZ&view=chart (accessed December 22, 2018).
12 See Gnanli Landrou, Coralie Brumaud, and Guillaume Habert, "Self-Compacting Clay Concrete: A Sustainable and Innovative Process to Build with Earth," *World Sustainable Built Environment Conference 2017: Hong Kong Conference Proceedings* (Hong Kong: Construction Industry Council, Hong Kong Green Building Council, June 5, 2017), pp. 1–7.
13 Michael Sorkin, "Architecture against Trump," open letter to the American Institute of Architects (November 12, 2016), https://worldarchitecture.org/articles/cgfch/_trump_presidency_represents_a_clear_danger_to_many_values_of_our_profession_says_michael_sorkin.html (accessed December 22, 2018).
14 India Block, "Elon Musk Reveals Plans to Create Bricks for Low-Cost Housing," *dezeen*, May 9, 2018, https://www.dezeen.com/2018/05/09/elon-musk-boring-company-earth-bricks/ (accessed September 11, 2018).
15 Farrokh Derakhshani, as cited in "Mud WORKS!" poster for the 15th International Architecture Exhibition, *Biennale architettura 2016: Reporting from the Front*, May 28 to November 27, 2016.
16 Henri Lefebvre, *The Survival of Capitalism*, translated by F. Bryant (London: Allison and Busby, 1976), as cited in David Pinder, "Reconstituting the Possible: Lefebvre, Utopia and the Urban Question," *International Journal of Urban and Regional Research*, 39, no. 1 (2015), pp. 28–45, here p. 36.

Opposite pages:

140 DESI Centre in Rudrapur, Bangladesh.
141 Ricola Kräuterzentrum in Basel, Switzerland.

142 Etosha House at the Basel Zoo, Switzerland.
143 Chapel of Reconciliation in Berlin, Germany.

144 Worms Cathedral altar in Germany.
145 Cupola at the ETH Zurich, Switzerland.

Author Biographies

Anna Heringer (*1977)
Architect and founder of Studio Anna Heringer, winner of numerous international distinctions including the Aga Khan Award, Obel Award, and Philippe Rotthier Prize for Architecture. Design critic at the Harvard University and visiting professorships at the University of Stuttgart, the University of Linz, and the Technical University Vienna. Guest lecturer at the ETH Zurich. UNESCO Honorary Professor of the Chair of Earthen Architecture, Building Cultures and Sustainable Development since 2010.

Lindsay Blair Howe (*1984)
Assistant Professor of Architecture and Society at the University of Liechtenstein. Studied and practiced architecture in Denmark, Germany, South Africa, Switzerland, and the United States. Interdisciplinary doctoral research in South Africa completed at the ETH Zurich Department of Architecture's Chair of Sociology in 2017. Former scientific and teaching assistant to Anna Heringer and Martin Rauch at the ETH Zurich.

Martin Rauch (*1958)
Founder of Lehm Ton Erde in Schlins, Austria, with more than thirty years of experience in earthen architecture and rammed earth construction worldwide. Numerous prizes, including a New European Bauhaus Award in 2021. Collaborations with institutions across Europe, the USA, Bangladesh, South Africa, and Egypt, such as Harvard University. Guest lecturer at the ETH Zurich. UNESCO Honorary Professor of the Chair of Earthen Architecture, Building Cultures and Sustainable Development since 2010.

The authors thank the many colleagues, friends, and students who contributed to the work behind this publication: Annette Spiro for the insightful introduction to this book; Dominique Gauzin-Müller for her instrumental guidance in earthen architecture and sustainable building; Veronika Darius for her invaluable support; Jürgen Laartz, Christian Keller, and Dirk Hebel for sharing their perspectives; and CRAterre, Amaco, Jean Dethier, and everyone associated with the UNESCO Chair of Earthen Architecture, Building Cultures and Sustainable Development. Special thanks are extended to Christian Schmitt, Wayne Switzer, and all of our former students and assistants at the ETH Zurich and beyond; and the passionate teams at the offices of Lehm Ton Erde and Studio Anna Heringer.

We also wish to thank the Ricola Foundation, Leeway Investment GmbH, Alnatura Produktions- und Handels GmbH, and the Land Vorarlberg for making this publication possible. Furthermore, we are grateful to the sponsors of the projects included in this book: Bundeskanzleramt Österreich; Cliff Curry and Delight Stone; ETH Zurich Department of Architecture; Eine Welt Gruppe Schlins; Land Vorarlberg; Lutz & Hedda Franz Charitable Trust; and OMICRON/Crossing Borders. Thanks are extended to the University of Liechtenstein for their support in this second edition.

Last but never least, thank you to our families, who inspire us to create a better world.

Illustration Credits

Iwan Baan, p. 135

Martina Bauer, p. 124 (right)

Simon Berger, p. 142 (bottom)

Karin Bleiweiss, p. 93

Julia Breu, p. 131

Beat Bühler, pp. 11–12, 77

Yannick Bühler, p. 142 (bottom)

Markus Bühler-Rasom, pp. 62–63

François Cointeraux, *École d'architecture rurale, ou Leçons par lesquelles on apprendra soi-même à bâtir solidement les maisons de plusieurs étages, avec la terre seule ou autres matériaux les plus communs et du plus vil prix* (Paris: l'Auteur, 1790), panels 6 and 10 (Bibliothèque nationale de France, Paris) p. 46

CRAterre, p. 49

Katharina Doblinger, p. 73

Marc Doradzillon, p. 91 (top)

Emmanuel Dorsaz, pp. 43 (right), 51–53, 116–117

Ralph Feiner, pp. 13, 81

Lea Frauenfelder, p. 138 (top left)

Anne de Henning/Aga Khan Trust for Culture, pp. 10, 22

Anna Heringer, pp. 41, 74 (left), 85 (top left, top right)

Heringer Rauch Nägele Waibel Naji, p. 85 (middle, bottom)

Kurt Hoerbst, pp. 28 (left), 31–32, 74 (right)

Naquib Hossain, p. 75

Lindsay Blair Howe, pp. 20, 34, 37, 43 (left), 131, 134, 136 (left)

Alexander Jaquermet, pp. 82–83

Blend Kader, p. 142 (bottom)

Karak, p. 84

Mathias Kestel, p. 99 (bottom left)

Bruno Klomfar, pp. 55, 69, 99 (top), 101, 129, 153

Nick Krouwel, p. 119 (left)

Jonas Landolt, p. 141

Pascal Lang, pp. 139 (left), 142 (bottom)

Lehm Ton Erde, pp. 87–89, 114, 132

Lu Lei, p. 36 (right)

Hanno Mackowitz, p. 104–107

Anna Maragkoudaki, p. 119 (right)

Stefano Mori, pp. 14–15, 94, 95 (top, bottom), 96 (right), 98, 99 (bottom right)

Gabrijela Obert, p. 103

Ender Özmen, p. 142 (bottom)

Dieter Petras, pp. 138 (bottom left), 139 (top right, bottom right), 142 (middle)

Pretoria Portland Cement Ltd., p. 25

Norbert Rau, pp. 123, 124 (left), 154

Johannes Rauch, p. 143

Martin Rauch, pp. 66–67, 95 (middle right), 96 (left)

Benedikt Redmann, pp. 17–18, 61, 151, 152

Gian Salis, pp. 56–58, 155

Kadir Sari, p. 142 (bottom)

Albrecht Imanuel Schnabel, pp. 78–79

Pauline Sémon, p. 95 (middle left)

Mara Simone, p. 142 (top)

Benjamin Stähli, p. 28 (right)

Leo Stieger, p. 36 (left)

Studio Anna Heringer, p. 49

Wayne Switzer, pp. 136 (right), 139 (top right, bottom right), 140

Team Rudrapur, pp. 71–72, 142

Jan Vogler, p. 142 (bottom)

Olaf Wiechers, p. 91 (bottom)

Copyediting
Thomas Skelton-Robinson, Zurich

Proofreading
Christopher Davey, Bolton, Connecticut

Graphic Design and Typesetting
Philippe Mouthon, Zurich

Image editing and printing
Offsetdruckerei Karl Grammlich GmbH, Pliezhausen

Fonts
Neue Haas Grotesk

Paper
Fly 07 (schneeweiss), spezialgeglättet, holzfrei, Volumen 1,2fach, 115g/m²

Cover Photograph
Bishop's Tomb, Sülchenkirche, Rottenburg, Germany. Architecture by Cukrowicz Nachbaur Architekten, 2015–2017. Photograph: Emmanuel Dorsaz.

© 2022, second, expanded edition,
gta Verlag, ETH Zurich
Institute for the History and Theory of Architecture
Department of Architecture
8093 Zurich, Switzerland
www.verlag.gta.arch.ethz.ch

© Texts by the authors
© Illustrations: by the image authors and their legal successors; for copyrights, see image credits

Every reasonable attempt has been made by the authors and publisher to identify owners of copyrights. Should any errors or omissions have occurred, please notify us.

The entire contents of this work, insofar as they do not affect the rights of third parties, are protected by copyright. All rights are reserved. No part of this publication may be reproduced, stored in a retrieval system, or transmitted, in any form or by any means, electronic, mechanical, photocopying, recording, or otherwise, without the written permission of the publisher.

The first edition of this publication was kindly supported by the Ricola Foundation, Leeway Investment GmbH, Alnatura Produktions- und Handels-GmbH, and the Land Vorarlberg. Thanks are extended to the University of Liechtenstein for their support in this second edition.

ISBN 978-3-85676-393-0